Neatly tucked within the eclectic South Austin neighborhood of Bouldin Creek, you'll find Thai Fresh—part gluten-free bakery, part coffeehouse, part vegan ice cream mecca and most importantly, part Thai restaurant and learning center. Since 2008, chef and owner Jam Sanitchat has been slowly building this culinary complex and teaching space, piecemeal style—expanding into neighboring spaces as they became available, forging loyal relationships with local growers and producers, and adding new facets to her culinary repertoire as time and money allowed. The result is a wildly successful amalgam of food, beverages and services that probably shouldn't work together, but somehow does.

Early on any given day, the coffeehouse, bakery and ice cream parlor side of Thai Fresh awakens to greet the morning crowd, filling the air over open laptops with the fragrant lure of roasted coffee beans and the sounds of grinders and dairy steamers. As the afternoon approaches, and the commuter traffic thins, the restaurant opens and the scene gives way to the lunch crowd trickling in on the other side of the building; the morning aromas and soundtrack quickly surrendering to the heady blasts of chilies, garlic, ginger and the hiss of charring meats. After a brief lull to catch breaths and restock, the dinner crowd shows up.

Jam's business model might be unconventional, but it clearly aligns with the modern Austin palate. There's deep love here for quality coffee and the coffeehouse experience, for craft products, for thoughtful and exciting cuisine spotlighting locally grown produce and sustainably raised meats, and for all things gluten-free and vegan. And the sometimes-fickle mixed bag of artists, families, downtown commuters, musicians, students, entrepreneurs and trendsetters that frequent Jam's place has not only established Thai Fresh as a neighborhood and hometown darling but also as a beckoning foodie destination for countless visitors who perhaps drifted into town for a music festival and became transfixed—their faces pressed against the candy-counter glass of our city. People come to Thai Fresh for Jam's delicious food, coffee, pastries and ice creams, but also for a glimpse of Austinites in the wild enjoying a very Austin-like establishment.

Those of us who've lived in this city long enough have watched Jam's passion for cooking and teaching blossom and grow. We've also been witness to her seemingly tireless dedication to the community—from donating food to countless nonprofit events and customers in need, to supporting urban farm programs and youth-outreach groups. This cookbook introduces us to the inspirations and people that instilled the core values that made Jam the chef she is today. And her delicious food acts as an edible memoir of the path thus far.

KIM LANE

We are PROUD to
partner with these
ranches,
farms & companies:
Coffee
Other

THAI FRESH

The Cookbook

Beloved Recipes from
a South Austin Icon

JAM SANITCHAT
with Kim Lane

Photographs by Jody Horton

This book is dedicated to my two late grandmothers, Ubon Wasuwat and Lan Sanitchat. You were the biggest part of my journey, and I am honored to have cooked by your side.

Contents

CHAPTER SIX

Foundational Elements 149

Sauces, Condiments and the Good Funk

CHAPTER SEVEN

Fusion Is Not a Dirty Word 171

Squid
Thai Fresh Hoodie
$36
Thai Fresh
organic tees
Coconut Cream
Coconut Milk

12100200
MASAMAN CURRY PASTE
N.W. 5.47 KGS.
G.W. 8.00 KGS.
DIM. 30.4x22.7x15.5 CM.
LOLA
C / No. 1-UP
12100202
N.W. 5.47 KGS.
G.W. 8.00 KGS.
KAREE CURRY PASTE
LOLA
C / No. 1-UP
12100208
N.W. 5.47 KGS.
G.W. 8.00 KGS.
DIM. 30.4x22.7x15.5 CM.
CURRY PASTE
Tapioca Starch
$1.35

Foreword

For as many obstacles as there are when opening a restaurant, there are even more to overcome keeping it running smoothly and successfully. But Thai Fresh founder and chef, Jam Sanitchat, has created and maintained a near perfect formula that most restaurateurs can only dream of. And she's managed to do it in a rapidly growing city with a food scene that's competitive, demanding and forever in flux. Not many eateries survive under such conditions, much less blossom and thrive the way Thai Fresh has.

I met Jam in 2005 when she was selling homemade Thai food at her farmers market stand in Austin. We connected instantly, and discovered that we shared similar passions, such as supporting local growers, eating healthily and preserving green space. This was well before "farm-to-table" had become an actual culinary movement in Austin, but Jam's deep commitment to local food was already evident. She'd begun incorporating fresh produce from fellow market vendors into her dishes, making them seasonally focused, popular with shoppers and uniquely relevant to time and place. She explained that this is how her family cooked in Thailand—using whatever was fresh at the market to plan their weekly meals. So, of course she carried this long-standing cultural tradition with her when she opened Thai Fresh in 2008.

Jam began her career at a time when the number of successful female chefs and restaurant owners in Austin were few and far between. And over the years, as our city rapidly grew into the food destination it is now, Jam morphed her business model to keep up with new demands and palates. Never afraid to challenge herself, she added vegan baked goods and dairy-free ice creams to the menu, and more recently, she increased her prices and removed the tip system in order to pay her staff a living wage. The move caught the attention of the editors at *Food & Wine* magazine, and they included Thai Fresh in their 2019 list of "Great Restaurants to Work For."

Jam has successfully created a multifaceted, welcoming space at Thai Fresh—one that reflects how she was raised, her deep love and appreciation for food and her strong belief in how it brings us together. This cookbook is a testament to what her loyal community already knows, and a great way for people from all over the world to get a little taste of what Jam and Thai Fresh have to offer.

SONYA COTÉ

Sonya Coté is the executive chef and owner of Eden East and Hillside Farmacy. She is a pioneer of the East Austin food scene, opening East Side Showroom in 2008. A champion of supporting local purveyors, Coté recognizes the importance of using locally grown ingredients for both nutritional and environmental benefits.

Introduction

When I was growing up, food was just as much a language spoken in my house as Thai. I come from a family of proud cooks; people who express their joys, celebrate successes and heal our family in tough times—always around a table. I learned to cook in this environment, at the knees of my grandmothers and mother near a wood-burning stove. I listened to them talk, I watched their hands, I memorized their techniques. This is where I learned that food is more than a basic necessity for life—it's a living thing. I learned that food not only connects us with our history, but it gives our lives context and a sense of place.

I discovered just how integral these things were to me when I moved to Austin to attend graduate school in 2001. I was very excited for the future, and I quickly fell in in love with my new city. But I was missing the comfort and support of an established, bonded community. Cooking my family's food made me feel better and tethered to something familiar. So that's what I did. I cooked for my roommates, schoolmates, dorm neighbors—basically anyone who stopped long enough to grab a spoon. I threw frequent dinner parties where every available space was covered with heaping platters of my family's language. It helped me feel like I was part of something bigger, and it opened the door to a path I didn't yet know I was about to follow.

After earning a degree from the University of Texas, I decided to try something completely different. I started a cottage business called "Thai Cooking with Jam," and began teaching people how to cook my family's recipes in their home kitchens. I also hosted classes in my own tiny kitchen, and I started a farmers market stand to sell my food and promote my classes. "Farm-to-table" was not yet a "thing," but at the market, I began to incorporate fellow vendors' seasonal, locally grown vegetables and fruits into my recipes—many of the ingredients uncommon to traditional Thai cuisine. I felt these new ingredients represented that context and sense of place that my mother and grandmothers had taught me was so important long ago. I brought my family's food to where I was in my life.

Almost two decades after moving to Austin, cooking and sharing food continue to be my passion. I opened Thai Fresh in 2008, and I've been teaching Thai cooking professionally for 16 years. I love to build confidence in people so they can take their new skills anywhere life takes them and make them their own just as I did. And the passion continues to grow! The Thai Fresh family is opening an ice cream shop on the eastside of Austin in early 2020. All ice creams are vegan and coconut-milk based and reflect the abundance of seasonal fruits available in Texas. I'm very excited to share this new venture with my beloved community.

When you eat my food, I'm telling you my story. Thank you for listening.

JAM SANITCHAT

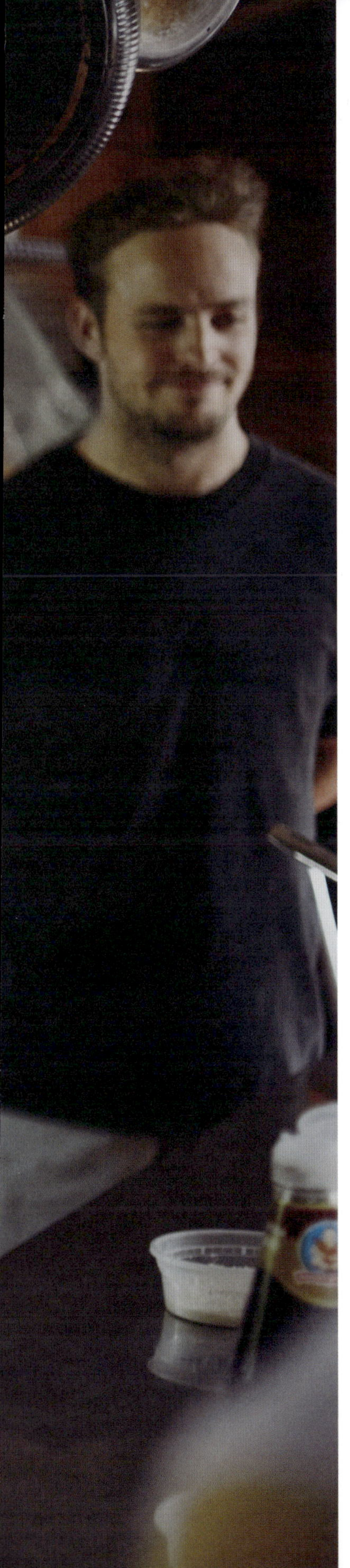

CHAPTER ONE

Jam's Master Class

I've been a cooking instructor for almost two decades, and I always begin my classes with some basic groundwork of Thai cuisine, to give students a sense of where we are headed together and why. Over the years, many of the same questions from students have arisen time and again. Consider this Master Class a compilation of answers. My hope is that it will give you a broader understanding of the unique elements, methods, techniques and fundamental flavors that set Thai cuisine apart.

พริกสด
ขีดละ-
10

Before We Begin

Balance

Thai cooking isn't especially difficult to learn, but there is a core principle to understand before you start: Something that is always present—*must be present*—for food to be considered authentic Thai is a balance of sweet, sour, salty, spicy and bitter flavors. This "five-flavor combo" balance is ancient to our culture and how we understand food. It's the only way we approach cooking.

This doesn't mean that each individual dish has to include all five flavors (though sometimes that's the case). It means that the entire meal itself represents a balance of all five flavors. Each flavor comes from different sources—for example, spicy can come from chili peppers, garlic, cloves or spices; sour from lime and lemon juices, fruits, vinegar and tamarind; sweet from sugars and fruits; salty from fish sauce, soy sauce or salt; and bitter from herbs, spices and even vegetables. A balanced representation of the five flavors in a meal satisfies all of your senses and makes you crave more.

I remember my grandmother and mom tasting their food as it was cooking. Whenever the taste was "off," they knew just what to add to find the balance. Sweet fixes sour and vice versa, they told me. Salt always tones down heat, and sugar will do the same. If you can break a dish down to its major flavor components, it will help you understand how to balance it with the other dishes on the table. While preparing food in my cooking classes, I invite students to taste the food after each ingredient is added—after the fish sauce or soy sauce, after the sugar, after the lime juice. This helps them grasp what's happening as the flavors develop.

Now that you understand the overall goal of finding balance, let's talk about the special methods, techniques and tools that will help get you there.

Methods

BRUISING

Bruising helps break down the fibrous parts of plants and spices, allowing the natural oils to be released. To bruise an ingredient, place it on a cutting board and whack it with a pestle, a meat mallet or the side of a heavy cleaver or knife. Use only moderate strength when bruising; the idea is to gently crush but not obliterate.

HEAT MAGIC

This is one of the first, and most important, techniques my grandmother taught me: Get the pan good and hot before you add the oil. Her words are still ringing in my ears: *"Don't put oil in the pan yet; it's not hot!"* I've heard some cooks recommend starting with a cool pan and warming the oil and the pan at the same time. But foods—especially eggs, proteins and starches like rice and noodles—tend to stick using this method. Preheating the pan to medium heat before *anything* goes in is the answer. Test the temperature of the pan by adding a few water droplets—they should immediately disappear. Right before you add the oil to the pan, lower the heat to medium-low. This will prevent the oil from getting too hot too fast, and prevent the spices from burning. Once you've lowered the heat and added the oil and spices, sauté until the spices are fragrant. Add other ingredients at this point and raise the heat back to medium or medium-high to continue cooking.

CHOOSING THE RIGHT OIL

Most of the time, Thais use vegetable oil to cook—specifically, soybean oil. It has a neutral taste and a high smoke-point suitable for Asian cooking. But any oil with a high smoke-point will work—like canola, grapeseed, safflower, sunflower or avocado. Avoid oils such as olive and coconut because of their lower smoke-point and strong flavors. And even though sesame oil has a high smoke-point, the flavor is so strong that we use it in very few recipes.

Tools

THE ALMIGHTY MORTAR AND PESTLE

I apologize in advance for pleading with you to purchase a mortar and pestle. I know it's a bulky request—especially if shelf space is precious—but I can't stress enough how foundational and important this tool is to Thai cuisine. Pounding and crushing ingredients does so much more for flavor development than simply chopping them with a sharp knife or using a food processor. Under the pestle, the cell walls of plants and herbs rupture, releasing the natural oils and liquids for a much deeper fragrance and flavor. Curry pastes become thick and rich, and spices are fully ground for optimum balance. Look for a heavy mortar that won't move around as you work, and one that's deep and wide enough to handle multiple ingredients as you build layers without sloshing bits all over your counter.

TEMPERATURE

Although I didn't grow up using thermometers, I've since come to find them indispensable. This is especially true when frying food because the temperature of the oil needs to remain constant for the food to cook properly and stay crisp and light. A good thermometer will also help you know when meat is cooked to the right temperature. A candy thermometer is handy when frying because it clips to the side of the pot. A stick thermometer works for both checking the internal temperature of meat and quickly checking heated oil.

A STIR-FRYING ESSENTIAL

A wok is an excellent tool to have in your kitchen arsenal if you have the right stove for it. A traditional round-bottom wok is designed to sit low on a gas burner, allowing the open flames to heat the sides. Food is cooked evenly and quickly because the wok captures heat throughout the entire surface area and distributes it as the food is moved around within. High heat is very important for cooking with a wok, so if you have a powerful gas burner of 12,000 BTUs or higher, a wok might be a good option for you. But is a wok essential to cooking Thai food? Not at all. Personally, I prefer to use a deep pan that's about 12 inches in diameter or wider, like a large frying pan, a Dutch oven or a deep, cast-iron or stainless-steel sauté pan. But because the majority of the heat will be concentrated in the bottom of the pan, it's trickier to stir-fry and get ingredients to cook evenly. That's why a Thai or Chinese spatula is an essential tool for stir-frying, whether you're using a wok or pan. The spatula has a long handle and a metal shovel to help you quickly stir and fold together a large quantity of ingredients at one time. It's also the perfect shape to scrape ingredients off the pan if they begin to stick.

A Thai spatula is an ideal tool for stir-frying.

Small Dried
Thai Chilies
Fresh Thai
Chilies
Dried Guajillo
Peppers

Special Ingredients

What Do They Bring?

The majority of ingredients used in this book are relatively common to the Western palate and readily available at most local grocers or Asian markets. However, there are a few items that might have a flavor profile unfamiliar to you, or that are harder to find (ordering online is a good option). Here's a quick look at what those ingredients bring to the table.

THAI CHILIES

Chili peppers are indispensable to authentic Thai cuisine. Unfortunately, many traditional Thai chili varieties are not easy to find in the U.S. (though many grow well here). Small red or green chilies—often labeled "Thai chilies" or "bird's eye chilies"—are bright, spicy and used frequently, either fresh or dried. You can usually find them at specialty grocery stores and at Asian markets, but failing that, substitute ¼ of a serrano pepper per chili in a recipe. Longer red or green chilies used in Thai cuisine are milder in heat with more fruit flavor, but difficult to find in the U.S. Anaheim, Holland, red jalapeños or Hatch peppers are a good substitute.

PANDAN LEAVES

The leaves from the tropical pandan plant have an earthy, vanilla aroma and flavor. They're most often used while cooking, then removed before serving. You can find them fresh and frozen at most Asian markets.

GALANGAL

A root-like underground stem (also known as a rhizome), galangal is a member of the ginger family and shares ginger's astringent, peppery flavor. Even when fresh, galangal can be woody, so it's often sliced into large coins for cooking, but removed before serving. It's edible, though (and delicious!), so mince or grind it if it's meant to be eaten in a dish. Galangal is available at some larger grocery stores and at Asian markets.

LEMONGRASS

A tropical stalk-like grass used in many Eastern cuisines, lemongrass has a citrusy, clean flavor. It often has woody outer layers that should be removed to reveal the tender interior stalk. In Thai cuisine, lemongrass is often added to a recipe in large pieces that have been bruised, then removed before serving. But it can be eaten as part of a dish if minced well or ground with a mortar and pestle. Many grocery stores now carry fresh lemongrass, but you can also find it at Asian markets.

CILANTRO ROOTS

Although using cilantro stems and leaves is fairly common in cuisines all over the world, using the roots of the plant is almost exclusive to Thailand. Cilantro roots are more aromatic and pungent than the stems or leaves, and have an earthy quality with hints of lemon and pepper. They might be hard to find at your local market, but the plant is easy to grow if you have a garden. They're usually available at Asian markets, and many farmers markets have begun to sell the entire plant. Minced cilantro stems can be substituted (3 stems per root) but won't be as pungent.

MAKRUT LIMES AND LEAVES

The makrut lime is a tropical fruit used in many Southeast Asian cuisines. It's similar to a standard lime but slightly more pungent and brighter in flavor. (Although both the juice and zest of the makrut lime are used in Thai cuisine, the leaves (fresh, dried or frozen) appear more often.) They impart an intense vegetal, citrus flavor but are usually not meant to be eaten unless they're cut into very small pieces. They can be found at most Asian markets.

HOLY BASIL

There are many varieties of basil, but holy basil is the one most commonly used for the recipes in this book. It's an intense and spicy herb with a peppery, clove-like bite and a slight mouth-numbing aftereffect. It lacks the sweetness and licorice flavor of its cousins, Thai basil and sweet basil. If you can't find holy basil, you can substitute Thai basil, lemon basil or sweet basil but it will dramatically change the flavor profile of the dish. (It will still be delicious, just different.) You can find holy basil at most Asian markets.

PALM SUGAR

Palm sugar is an unrefined sugar made from the sap of the coconut palm tree. In Thai cuisine, it's used in both savory and sweet dishes for its rich, complex, maple-like flavor. You can find it at most larger grocery stores and at Asian markets.

BROWNED GARLIC

This is one of the most questioned ingredients/techniques in my cooking classes. Many students have heard that garlic becomes bitter when browned, or that it's burning as soon as it begins to brown. Untrue! When you brown garlic, it caramelizes and becomes sweet. It's an important first step in Thai stir-fries, so don't be afraid! Just make sure that your pan is hot before adding the oil. Once the oil goes in, immediately turn the heat to low before adding the garlic to prevent it from cooking too fast. Let the garlic crisp around the edges and turn golden brown. You're now ready to add the next ingredients.

Makrut Lime
Leaves
Lemongrass
Galangal

Tamarind
Pulp
Tamarind
Water

FISH SAUCE

Fish sauce is a crucial flavor in Thai cuisine. It adds a briny, meaty umami to foods, but beware: It doesn't smell so great to the Western nose. The key is to use a high-quality fish sauce with a high protein level (the protein is pure flavor). You'll pay more for it, but it will make a huge difference in taste. For vegetarians, substitute light Thai soy sauce, but use 20% less because of the salt content.

TAMARIND WATER

Tamarind is a pod-like, tart/sweet fruit that's commonly used in the cuisines of Southeast Asia, India, Africa, Mexico and others. It can pack a serious pucker, so a little goes a long way. In Thai cuisine, we often use tamarind water (basically, diluted tamarind concentrate). I like to make tamarind water using a block of dried, seedless tamarind pulp found at Asian markets. (A block lasts a long time and doesn't require refrigeration.) Make the tamarind water in two batches to get all of the tamarind flavor out of the pulp. In a bowl, soak ⅓ cup dried, seedless tamarind pulp in ¾ cup of water for 10 to 15 minutes to let the fruit soften. Working with your fingers, break up the tamarind until the water thickens slightly. Use a fine-mesh strainer to strain the thick water into a separate container (reserving the tamarind solids in the bowl) and set aside (see left). Add another ¾ cup of water to the tamarind solids in the bowl and repeat the mixing process. Strain the second batch of water and combine it with the first (discarding the tamarind solids). The water should be the consistency of thin gravy or muddy water. If the water is too thin, add more seedless tamarind and repeat the process. If the water is very thick, add more water. Store any unused portion in the refrigerator for up to a week.

GLUTEN-FREE SOY SAUCES

Gluten-free soy sauces can be hard to find. Bragg Liquid Aminos is a good substitute, or you can make your own gluten-free light or dark soy sauce by using these recipes.

FOR GLUTEN-FREE LIGHT SOY SAUCE:

½ c. gluten-free tamari sauce

1 ½ c. water

2 T. plus 2t. salt

2 T. sugar

FOR GLUTEN-FREE DARK SOY SAUCE:

1 c. gluten-free light soy sauce recipe

1 T. molasses

½ c. sugar

ข้าวเสาไห้
โลละ 28
ถังละ 400

Jasmine Rice

MAKES 6 CUPS

Thais have been growing, harvesting and cooking rice for centuries—it's basically the backbone of our cuisine and culture. In Thailand, we mainly use jasmine rice for recipes that call for "white rice." My cooking method for jasmine rice has been tested over and over and over—I promise it will yield perfect results on the stovetop. No more mushy rice or burning the bottom of the pot! By all means, use a rice cooker if you have one—it makes the process even easier! But rest assured, you can make perfect rice without it. Here's the secret: Most people use too much water to cook rice. Even the instructions on the bag are wrong! Contrary to the accepted formula of a 1:2 rice-to-water ratio, this recipe calls for a 1:1½ ratio. (If you're making regular long-grain rice or basmati rice, you might need to add a little more water, like a 1:1¾ rice-to-water ratio. But jasmine rice has more moisture, so it requires less water.)

3 c. jasmine rice
4 ½ c. water

Add the rice and water to a pot. The rule of thumb here is that the level of rice and water should never come up higher than half the pot. So, for this batch, use a 2-quart-size (or larger) pot with a lid. Stir the rice with your hand and level the rice. Bring the water to a boil and then turn down the heat as low as it will go. Put the lid on the pot and let the rice cook for 12 minutes. Turn off the heat and let the rice sit, covered, for about 10 more minutes. Fluff with a fork and serve.

Boiled Rice

MAKES 6 CUPS

Unlike steamed rice, where the cooked rice kernels retain their shape and a bit of tooth, boiled rice produces plump, pillow-y kernels that have opened and will eventually quadruple in size—that's what we're looking for! This rice is usually served family-style with a variety of fried, pickled, stir-fried and boiled dishes on the side for mixing and matching. Salted Duck Eggs (p. 152) are a particular pairing favorite, but the Candied Pork Belly (p. 163), Fried Beef Jerky (p. 142) or Thai Omelet Breakfast Taco (p. 197) would also be delicious. Boiled rice will keep for several days in the fridge. When reheating, add a bit of water to moisten.

2 c. jasmine rice
6 c. water (more, if needed)
Pinch salt

Bring all of the ingredients to a boil. Reduce the heat and simmer for 15 to 20 minutes, uncovered, until the rice kernels open.

Brown Rice

MAKES 6 CUPS

My dad gets the credit for this brown rice cooking method. Brown rice is not very common in Thai culture—we are quite literally "white-on-rice" folks. But over the past 20 years, it's become more popular because of its health benefits (high fiber, vitamins, antioxidants, etc.). My dad, who would never eat brown rice when I was growing up, suddenly got into making it and eventually perfected this method. By all means, use a rice-cooker if you have one. Just wait for the rice to soak before you push the button to steam.

3 c. brown rice

4 ½ c. water

Add the rice and water to a pot. The rule of thumb is that the level of rice and water should never come up higher than half the pot. So, for this batch, use a 2-quart-size pot with a lid. Let the rice soak for 30 minutes. (If you cook brown rice without soaking it first, it requires more water and a longer cook time, causing the rice to become mushy.) Bring the water to a boil, then turn down the heat as low as your stove will go. Put the lid on the pot and cook the rice, covered, for 15 minutes. Turn off the heat and let the rice sit, covered, for another 10 minutes. Fluff with a fork and serve.

Coconut Rice

MAKES 4 CUPS

I usually serve Coconut Rice with Papaya Salad (p. 125), but I've also served it with Southern-Thai-Style Grilled Chicken (p. 130) and Massaman Curry (p. 180). It's creamier and a tad sweeter than just plain rice, and it's made using something called "old-crop" jasmine rice, which has less moisture than a newer crop. In Thailand, you can specify if you want to buy older or newer rice. I would say old-crop is like aged rice because it cooks up more grain-like rather than mushy. In the U.S., a bag of rice sometimes states if it's new-crop, but sometimes not. You can substitute a mix of jasmine rice and regular long-grain rice (which has less moisture) for a similar effect.

2 c. coconut cream

1 c. water

1 t. salt

2 t. sugar

2 c. old-crop jasmine rice (or a combo of jasmine and long grain rice)

3 pandan leaves

Fried shallots (p. 168), for topping (optional)

In a lidded pot, combine the coconut cream, water, salt and sugar, and stir to dissolve. Add the rice and stir well. Massage the pandan leaves a few times to release oils, then break them into large pieces (to be removed later) and add them to the rice. Bring the pot to a boil, turn down the heat to a very low simmer, cover and cook for 10 minutes. Uncover and stir the rice so the cream and rice are well mixed. With a large spoon, rotate the rice from the bottom of the pot to the top. Cover and cook for another 5 minutes. Turn off the heat and let stand, covered, for another 10 minutes. Remove the pandan leaves and top with the fried shallots, if using.

Sticky Rice

MAKES 6 CUPS

Sticky rice, usually labeled "sweet rice" or "glutinous rice" (though it contains no gluten) is most common in the north and northeastern areas of Thailand. It's eaten with various street-food dishes—usually Papaya Salad (p. 125), grilled chicken, fried foods and larb—but also with everything from curries and salads to stir-fries. Because you can easily form the rice into a bite with your fingers, it's meant to be eaten without a utensil. Sticky rice is easy to prepare and keeps well. When reheating, just sprinkle on a little bit of water to help moisten it, then steam for a minute or two.

2 c. long-grain sweet rice
Water, to cover

In a large pot, soak the sweet rice for 4 hours in water that's about 6 inches above the surface of the rice. (It can be soaked up to 8 to 12 hours without being oversoaked.) Drain and set aside. Add water to the bottom section of a steamer and bring to a boil. Lower the heat to a low simmer, place the rice in the top part of the steamer and set over the simmering water. Put the lid on the steamer and cook the rice for 15 minutes. When the rice is done, it should be completely opaque. If there are still some spots of white on the grains of rice, steam in 5-minute increments until opaque. As an alternative to traditional steaming, place a damp kitchen towel over a plate that fits in the microwave. Spread the soaked rice over the towel and fold in the sides so that the rice is completely covered. Put the plate in the microwave and cook on high for 3 minutes. Check to see if the rice is opaque. If it's not, continue to cook in 1-minute increments until opaque. Regardless of cooking method, serve immediately or cool completely and store in the fridge for up to a week.

Red Curry Paste

MAKES ½ CUP

- 1 t. chopped galangal
- 1 T. chopped lemongrass
- 5 large dried Thai red peppers, seeded and soaked for 20 minutes in warm water, then chopped
- 7 garlic cloves
- 2 shallots, chopped
- 1 t. makrut lime zest
- 2 t. chopped cilantro stems
- 5 black peppercorns
- 1 t. salt

Using a mortar and pestle, pound 1 ingredient at a time in the order listed until it's mostly ground. Then add the next and so on. Alternatively, double the amount of the ingredients and use a powerful blender, like a Vitamix, to make the paste. The paste can be stored in the refrigerator for up to 1 month, but do not freeze.

**If you don't have time to make homemade curry paste, I recommend the Maesri brand as a good substitute.*

Yellow Curry Paste

MAKES ½ CUP

- 1 T. coriander seeds
- 1 T. cumin seeds
- 1 t. minced galangal
- 1 T. thinly sliced lemongrass
- 1 t. chopped ginger
- 3 dried Thai red chilies, soaked in cold water, then seeded
- ¼ c. chopped shallots
- 6 garlic cloves, chopped
- 1 t. salt
- 2 T. curry powder (often labeled "yellow" or "Indian" curry powder)
- 1 t. shrimp paste

Toast the coriander seeds, cumin seeds and galangal separately in a dry pan over medium heat. Move 1 ingredient around until fragrant, then remove and toast the next. After the dried spices are toasted and removed, toast the lemongrass and ginger together, then remove. Finally, toast the chilies, shallots and garlic together, then remove. Using a large mortar and pestle, add 1 ingredient at a time—beginning with the seeds—in the order listed. Pound each ingredient until it's mostly ground before adding the next. When you get to the chilies, shallots and garlic, add the salt and pound (the salt helps absorb moisture and prevent splattering). Finally, add the curry powder and shrimp paste. Alternatively, double the amount of the ingredients and use a powerful blender, like a Vitamix. The paste can be stored in the refrigerator for up to 1 month, but do not freeze.

Green Curry Paste

MAKES ½ CUP

½ t. coriander seeds
¼ t. cumin seeds
1 t. white peppercorns
1 T. peeled, finely minced galangal
Large pinch salt
2 T. finely minced lemongrass (about 2 stalk)
10–15 small, green Thai chilies, roughly chopped
1 T. finely minced makrut lime zest
2 t. chopped cilantro roots or stems
2 T. chopped shallots
1 T. minced garlic
1 t. shrimp paste

Toast the coriander seeds by heating a dry frying pan over medium-low heat. Add the coriander seeds to the pan and move them around constantly until fragrant and lightly browned—about 1 to 2 minutes. Remove to a small bowl. Next, add the cumin seeds to the pan and heat until fragrant and lightly browned. Add them to a separate small bowl and set aside (the coriander and cumin seeds need to be toasted separately because they toast at different rates). Using a large mortar and pestle, make a paste by adding the ingredients, 1 at a time, in the order given. Pound 1 ingredient until it's broken into small pieces before adding the next 1. When all of the ingredients have been added, continue pounding until the mix forms a fine paste. The paste can be stored in the refrigerator for up to 1 month, but do not freeze.

Massaman Curry Paste

MAKES ABOUT ½ CUP

3 shallots
2 garlic cloves
1 t. coriander seeds
1 t. cumin seeds
2 whole cloves
5 large dried red Thai chilies, seeded, soaked in warm water for 20 minutes, chopped
1 t. salt
1 t. ground white pepper
1 T. chopped lemongrass
1 T. finely chopped galangal
1 t. makrut lime zest (optional)
2 t. chopped cilantro
1 t. shrimp paste

Place the shallots and garlic cloves on a small baking pan and roast in the oven at 350º until slightly charred. Set aside. Toast the coriander seeds by heating a dry frying pan over medium-low heat. Add the coriander seeds to the pan and move them around constantly until fragrant and lightly browned—about 1 to 2 minutes. Remove to a small bowl. Next, add the cumin seeds to the pan and heat until fragrant and lightly browned. Remove them to a separate small bowl and set aside (the coriander and cumin seeds need to be toasted separately because they toast at different rates). Next, toast the cloves until fragrant and remove to another bowl. Using a large mortar and pestle, make a paste by adding the ingredients one at a time, beginning with the seeds and cloves. Continue with the shallots, garlic cloves and chilies—pounding each ingredient until it's broken into small pieces before adding the next one. Continue with the rest of the ingredients until the mix forms a fine paste.

Panang Curry Paste

MAKES ABOUT 2 CUPS

½ c. peanuts

½ t. cumin seeds

½ t. coriander seeds

1 piece nutmeg (about ⅛ of a whole nutmeg)

1 T. minced lemongrass

1½ T. minced galangal

10 large dried red Thai chilies, seeded, soaked for 20 minutes in warm water, chopped

¼ c. chopped shallots

10 garlic cloves, chopped

1 t. salt

1 t. makrut lime zest

1 t. minced cilantro roots (or 5 cilantro stems, minced)

1 t. shrimp paste

Roast the peanuts on a sheet pan in a 325º oven until fragrant and slightly golden. When cool, chop, measure out 4 tablespoons and set aside. Toast the cumin seeds, coriander seeds and nutmeg separately in a dry pan over medium heat. Move 1 ingredient around until fragrant, then remove and toast the next. Using a large mortar and pestle, pound 1 ingredient at a time—beginning with the roasted peanuts and toasted seeds—in the order listed. Pound each ingredient until it's mostly ground before adding the next. When you get to the chilies, shallots and garlic, add the salt and pound (the salt helps absorb moisture and prevent splattering). Finally, add the lime zest, cilantro and shrimp paste. (Alternatively, double the amount of the ingredients and use a powerful blender, like a Vitamix.) The paste can be stored in the refrigerator for up to 1 month, but do not freeze.

**If you don't have time to make homemade curry paste, I recommend the Maesri brand as a good substitute for all these curry recipes.*

Cooking with Tofu

Tofu adds wonderful texture and heft to recipes, but honestly, it's flavorless and can be a bit intimidating to work with for someone unfamiliar with its properties. If you'd like to include tofu in any of the recipes in this book, I suggest using firm or extra-firm tofu, which is more forgiving and able to hold up better in stir-fries and during longer cooking times.

PRESSING TOFU

The first thing we need to do is reduce the water content in the tofu. (Without removing water, the tofu won't be able to absorb flavors or sauces.) To do this, place the tofu block on a dry, clean kitchen towel spread over a cutting board. Place another dry, clean towel over the tofu and fold in the sides so it's a little bigger than the tofu block. Place a heavy object like a pot on top of the covered tofu and let it press for 30 minutes. (Make sure the pot isn't too heavy or it might break the tofu.)

FREEZING / THAWING TOFU

Another way to remove water from tofu is to freeze and then thaw it. To do this, place the newly opened tofu block on a plate and into the freezer. One hour before using, remove the tofu from the freezer and place on a dry, clean kitchen towel to thaw. The frozen water in the tofu will melt out, leaving just the porous tofu with a meaty texture. When using this method, there's no need to fry or bake the cubes afterward, unless a recipe calls for it or you just really want to. They're ready to soak up your delicious stir-fry flavors and curries, as is.

FRYING TOFU

Thoroughly pressing and draining tofu is especially important if you plan to fry it. Fried tofu holds together well, has a dense texture and still absorbs the flavors and sauces in your recipes even though fried. You'll see fried tofu cubes added to dishes like my Coconut Vermicelli (p. 133) and Pad Thai (p. 119). Of course, frying tofu (or anything, really) can be a little intimidating—my students often tell me how nervous it makes them. Key strategies are to use thoroughly dry tofu, to fry at the right temperature (350º) and to keep the process as hassle-free as possible. Even the smallest deep fryer will make the process so much easier, but I often bypass the deep fryer altogether and use a small- to medium-size pot. And there's no need to discard the oil afterward. Let it cool, use a fine-mesh strainer to get rid of any solids and reuse the oil in other recipes. Now let's get frying!

Cut the pressed tofu into 1-inch cubes. Fill a pot or deep fryer with vegetable oil to about 6 inches above the bottom of the pot. (If using a smaller pot, you won't need as much oil, but you will have to fry the cubes in several batches.) Heat the oil to 350º. Using tongs or a spoon, slowly lower enough of the cubes into the oil to create 1 layer. Let the cubes fry for about 5 minutes—moving them around occasionally with the tongs—until they're golden and starting to float. Remove the cubes to a paper towel-lined platter and repeat until all of the tofu is fried.

BAKING TOFU

If frying the tofu cubes seems like too much of a hassle, you can always bake them. Simply toss 1 pound of tofu cubes in 2 tablespoons vegetable oil mixed with 1 tablespoon soy sauce. (Soy sauce is added for a little flavor boost since baking the cubes won't create the same super-dry texture as frying.) Place the cubes on a baking rack over a sheet pan and bake at 350º for about 15 minutes, or until your desired texture is achieved.

Fried tofu cubes.

Pairing Wine with Thai Food

By Rae Wilson

Most wine experts agree that the vibrant range of fresh herbs, bright citrus, rich coconut milk and often blistering heat present in Thai cuisine typically balances well with a lightly sweet, unoaked white or a dry rosé. Of course, there's always room for a little stretching—think younger, fruitier reds with low tannins, such as pinot noir, Zinfandel or sangiovese, and don't forget sparkling wines! When pairing wine with Thai food, it's best to keep in mind the broader components and major flavor profiles present in any dish. Here, we've split those major components into four categories and suggested diverse wines to complement the array of textures and flavors.

RICH AND CREAMY

From silky soups to spicy curries, coconut milk-based dishes lend themselves to lightly sweet wines like pinot gris and those with a dry finish like grenache blanc. Flowery and tropical viognier and warm-weather chardonnays also work well to balance creamy dishes that contain a lightly sour aspect as well. But when in doubt, a traditional dry rosé is the perfect choice for the majority of coconut milk-based sauces.

Based in Austin, Texas, Rae Wilson is the founder/winemaker of Wine for the People. From her roots as a sommelier, Rae turned her focus to winemaking in Napa Valley, Portugal and later, Texas. She currently has three wine productions and a dog named Amos.

FIRE AND SPICE

Spicy Thai dishes are at the epicenter of this cuisine's most classic wine pairings. Lightly sweet and off-dry rieslings dominate the category, but an off-dry chenin blanc would also be an excellent choice. If you prefer red wine, a soft, fruity grape such as a pinot noir, a young sangiovese or even a silky grenache are excellent choices to complement heat.

CITRUSY AND HERBACEOUS

Bright citrus and herb-heavy dishes work well with wines like a richly textured sémillon, a fresh albariño or a dry rosé. With its mineral and white-pepper notes, grüner veltliner riesling is another choice to consider. And a skin-contact white, like a ramato pinot grigio, will harmonize with any sharp citrus tones.

STIR-FRIED AND DEEP-FRIED

Unfortunately, sparkling wines tend to be lumped into the category of "special occasion," but their pairing potential shouldn't be overlooked when it comes to fried foods. Fried rice dishes and stir-fried meats and vegetables get a lift in spirit from the fizz and fruit, and heavier, breaded and crunchy foods benefit from a lightweight, off-dry profile. Favorites include sparkling chenin blanc, riesling and rosé.

Mujeres

CHAPTER TWO

When We Gather

People gathered around large, communal plates of food is a common sight in Thailand. Food is our way to connect, catch up, show love and respect and celebrate *everything*: birthdays, a change in season, a new baby, a bountiful rice harvest—the list goes on. So, preparing and sharing food was a natural way to show appreciation for the new friendships I made when I moved to this country. Even though everything was new and foreign to me, familiar food from my homeland remained my constant comfort—reminding me that I was loved, missed and appreciated. Here are my go-to recipes to feed family and friends, and they're great for dinner parties because they keep well on the table as people talk, laugh and mingle. Sharing food is much more than simply fulfilling one of life's basic needs—it's truly life itself.

Green Curry with Sirloin and Summer Squash

SERVES 4

Green curry is one of the spiciest curries in Thai cooking and my mom's favorite. I remember helping her make it as a kid, and when I moved to the U.S., it was one of the curries that I knew how to make by heart. I made this dish several times at gatherings as a graduate student, and wherever that pot was located in the house, people tended to drift to it and gather around—it's definitely a crowd-pleaser. Green Curry Paste (p. 42) uses small, fresh, green Thai chilies, which give it a vivid, verdant color and hefty bite. Sometimes cooks add chili leaves to intensify the green or larger Thai green chilies to maintain the color but tame the heat a bit. If you have any leftovers, use them to make Green Curry Fried Rice (p. 80).

2 13 ½-oz. unshaken cans coconut milk

½ c. Green Curry Paste (p. 42)

1 ½ lb. beef sirloin, sliced across the grain into 1-inch × 1½-inch pieces about ⅛-inch thick

½ c. water

4 c. chopped summer squash (or other firm vegetables)

3–4 T. fish sauce

2 t. sugar

3 makrut lime leaves, torn

1 c. Thai basil leaves, whole

SUGGESTED WINE:

OREGON PINOT GRIS

Do not shake the coconut milk. Open the cans and gently scoop the cream off the top, going about halfway down each can. As you near halfway, the cream will get lighter in consistency—that's okay! Just go all the way to half for a half-can's worth of cream and liquid. In a large saucepot, bring the cream to a boil over medium heat. Boil the cream for 1 minute, then stir in the curry paste and mix until smooth. Reduce the heat to a simmer and cook, without stirring, until the mixture is fragrant and the coconut cream starts to release some oil—about 3 to 5 minutes. Add the beef to the mixture and simmer for 5 minutes—stirring occasionally every 30 seconds or so. Add the remaining coconut milk and water and return the mixture to a boil. After it boils, reduce the heat to a low simmer and cook the beef for 30 minutes. Add the squash and bring the mixture back to a boil, then reduce the heat and let it simmer for 2 to 3 minutes over low heat. Season with the fish sauce and sugar. Taste for seasoning, then add the Thai basil and makrut lime leaves and turn off the heat.

Spicy Glass Noodle Salad

SERVES 2

Growing up in a family of great cooks, I ended up helping out a lot in the kitchen. I never got the chance to be completely in charge of a full meal, though. Instead, I helped chop vegetables, made curry paste, grabbed things, picked some herbs in the garden, etc. However, with this Spicy Glass Noodle Salad, I can confidently say that I played an important part in perfecting the final outcome and making it my own. Over time, I discovered that a pork-and-shrimp combo was the most palate-pleasing, and that mincing the meat very finely helped distribute the flavors and textures more evenly into the dish. "That way, there's meat in every bite," Mom would say. I remember feeling like the "important cook" every time I made this dish for my family (while Mom was respectfully relegated to sous-chef duties, at least for this dish). Spicy Glass Noodle Salad is perfect for a leisurely family dinner or a laid-back gathering with friends, because it holds very well for hours at room temperature. It does have a kick, though, so adjust the spiciness to your taste. You can make this dish vegetarian by substituting your favorite soybean protein and mushrooms for the shrimp and pork in the salad, and by substituting soy sauce for the fish sauce in the dressing.

FOR THE DRESSING:

1–2 small fresh Thai chilies, minced

1 t. white sugar

2 t. palm sugar

¼ c. lime juice

3 T. fish sauce

FOR THE SALAD:

8 oz. dried glass noodles (also known as cellophane or bean thread noodles)

2 T. vegetable oil

2 garlic cloves, minced

¼ lb. ground pork

¼ lb. shelled, deveined shrimp, minced well

1 T. soy sauce, or to taste

2 T. water

2 tomatoes, chopped

¼ c. chopped cilantro

1–2 shallots, sliced thinly

2 green onions, both green and white parts, cut into ⅛-inch pieces

SUGGESTED WINE:

SPANISH ALBARIÑO

Make the dressing by whisking all of the ingredients together.

Soak the noodles in cold tap water for 30 minutes, then place in boiling water for 10 seconds, drain and set aside. Heat the oil in a sauté pan over medium heat. Add the garlic and fry until fragrant and slightly brown. Add the pork (breaking it into very small pieces as you add) and shrimp and stir occasionally until cooked—about 2 minutes. Add the soy sauce and water and turn off the heat. Place the meat mixture, the noodles and the rest of the ingredients in a large mixing bowl. Pour the dressing on the salad a little bit at a time and mix well between additions. Taste and add more dressing, if desired.

Tom Yum Talay

Spicy Mixed-Seafood Soup with Salty-Sour Finishing Sauce

SERVES 2

Tom Yum, or lemongrass soup, is one of the most popular dishes in Thailand. Almost every time we ate out as a family, my dad ordered a big pot for the table to share. My version below includes seafood, and you can make it with or without the Thai Chili Jam (p. 153) and fried Thai chilies, but adding them brings a more complex flavor profile to the soup. Make a big pot, set it out and let your guests serve themselves.

FOR THE FINISHING SAUCE:

4 T. lime juice

2–3 small, fresh Thai chilies, red or green, minced

3 T. fish sauce

1 t. sugar

¼ c. rough-chopped cilantro stems

FOR THE SOUP:

4 c. fish stock, Chicken Stock (p. 150) or water

1 stalk lemongrass, tough outer layer removed, bruised with the back of a knife, cut into 1½-inch thick pieces

4 ⅛-inch-thick galangal slices, bruised with the back of the knife

1 T. fish sauce

4 makrut lime leaves, torn into smaller pieces (do not shred)

4 large shrimp with shells, heads on, if possible (shelled and headless will work, but the shells and heads add a lot of flavor to the stock)

6 mussels, shelled

2 sea scallops, chopped into bite-size pieces

4 c. shiitake, oyster or button mushrooms, sliced

3 small dried Thai chilies, fried

1 T. Thai Chili Jam (p. 153)

To make the sauce, combine all of the ingredients in a bowl, whisk to dissolve the sugar and set aside.

To make the soup, bring the stock to a boil in a large pot. Add the lemongrass, galangal, fish sauce and lime leaves. Let simmer for 1 minute. Add the seafood and the mushrooms. Lower the heat to a simmer and cook for about 2 minutes. Meanwhile, fry the dried Thai chilies in a small skillet with a splash of vegetable oil until fragrant and darker in color. Add the fried chilies to the soup along with the Thai Chili Jam and stir to combine. Turn off the heat, pour the finishing sauce over the soup, stir it in and serve. Remind guests to remove or eat around the lemongrass, galangal and lime leaves.

Pineapple Fried Rice with Shrimp

SERVES 4–6

This is another perfect example of the "five-flavor combo" (p. 27) that appears repeatedly in Thai cuisine. The curry powder works beautifully with the sweet and sour flavors of the pineapple. (Even though curry powder is of Indian origin, it's used widely in Thai cuisine.) This is the dish we would order as a family when we would go out to eat in Thailand. At restaurants, the rice is usually presented in a hollowed-out pineapple—so pretty! This rice feeds a crowd, so feel free to scale it back for your needs. And be sure to use day-old cooked rice instead of freshly made rice, which doesn't hold up well to frying.

¼ c. plus 2 T. vegetable oil
4 garlic cloves, minced
20 medium shrimp, peeled, deveined
½ t. salt
2 T. yellow curry powder
1 c. chopped yellow onion
4 eggs
1 c. minced fresh or frozen pineapple
6 c. cooked jasmine rice (p. 37)
4 T. light soy sauce
2 T. white sugar
¼ c. chopped spring onions (green parts only), about 1½-inch long pieces
2 T. cilantro leaves, for garnish

Heat a very large, deep sauté pan over medium heat. Add the oil and when it shimmers, fry the garlic until fragrant and just starting to brown, about 10 seconds. Turn the heat to low and add the shrimp, salt, curry powder and onions. Turn the heat back to medium and stir-fry until the shrimp are almost cooked, about 1 minute. Push the mixture in the pan to the sides, crack in the eggs and lightly scramble (not all the way). Let the mixture fry without stirring for 1 minute. Add the pineapple, fold in the rice and mix. Add the soy sauce and sugar and mix for about 30 more seconds to let the sugar dissolve. Taste and adjust the seasoning, if needed. Fold in the green onions and turn off the heat. Garnish with the cilantro and serve.

PRO TIP

It's Okay to Brown

Browning the garlic caramelizes the natural sugars and deepens the flavor.

Mom's Chicken Rice

CUSTOMER FAVORITE — RECIPE —

SERVES 8–10

Chicken Rice is a staple of Thailand's street-food culture. Growing up, my family would often go out seeking the best version we could find. My mom didn't start making the dish at home until about midway through my elementary school years, and I remember her version just seemed to appear all of a sudden, without any of the expected recipe trial and error. We didn't ask questions, though, because her Chicken Rice was perfect—incredibly delicious and fragrant. The best part was her sauce. No one—not even Thailand's most famous Chicken Rice restaurants—could surpass her sauce. It definitely became the family favorite, and a favorite of friends, too. In fact, Mom made the dish in Australia when she was an exchange teacher there and a close friend from that trip showed up on our doorstep one day, a whole chicken in his hands, and begged Mom to make the dish for him again. Years later, she revealed that the recipe had actually come from a friend. Apparently, the friend had borrowed some money from Mom and couldn't quite pay it back. So, Mom told her, *"If you give me that Chicken Rice recipe, I'll just forget about the money."* That was money well spent.

I brought Mom's recipe with me when I came to the U.S., but I still had to call her in Thailand in the middle of the night to walk me through the process. Chicken Rice was one of the very first dishes I made to impress friends, and I guess it deserves some of the credit for all of the new friendships I've made over the years, because friends and their friends keep requesting it over and over at my dinner parties. Mom's Chicken Rice definitely started my love of cooking and put me on the path to becoming a chef.

FOR THE CHICKEN AND STOCK:

1 whole chicken (about 3 lb.)

3 garlic cloves, crushed

10 cilantro stems

5 ginger slices (¼-inch thick)

2 t. salt

FOR THE RICE:

¼ c. chicken fat (or substitute vegetable oil)

2 T. finely chopped garlic

2 T. finely chopped ginger

1 T. finely chopped cilantro stems (or, if you have cilantro roots, use 1 chopped root)

6 c. uncooked jasmine rice

8 c. reserved chicken stock, divided

(continued on following page)

To make the chicken and stock, place all of the ingredients in a large stockpot and add enough water just to cover. Bring to a boil, then reduce the heat to low, cover and let simmer for 25 minutes. After 25 minutes, remove the chicken to a platter to cool. Pour the stock through a fine-mesh strainer, discard the solids and set the stock aside. When the chicken is cool enough to handle, pull and/or slice the meat from the bones. Cover the meat to keep it from drying out and set aside. You may not need to use all the stock for this recipe, so refrigerate or freeze the excess.

To make the rice, heat the chicken fat or oil in a large skillet over medium heat. Add the garlic, ginger and cilantro stems and fry until fragrant and golden brown. Add the rice and fry for about a minute. Add ½ cup of the stock and continue to stir-fry until the rice is golden brown—about 1 minute. Transfer the rice mixture to a large pot, add the remaining 7½ cups of stock, and stir to mix and level the rice. Bring to a boil, lower the heat to a simmer and cover with a lid or foil until the rice is cooked—about 15 minutes.

FOR THE SAUCE:

2 T. finely chopped ginger

2 T. finely chopped garlic

2 T. finely chopped fresh Thai chilis

1⅓ c. light soy sauce

¼ c. dark soy sauce

¼ c. soybean paste

¼ c. granulated sugar

¼ c. lime juice

¼ c. water

½ c. white vinegar

FOR GARNISH/SERVING:

½ c. fresh cilantro leaves

3 sliced cucumbers

To make the sauce, combine all of the ingredients. Taste and adjust seasonings, if needed. To serve, place the rice on a large serving platter, top with the chicken meat and garnish with the fresh cilantro leaves. Serve the sauce on the side in a large bowl with a spoon so guests can sauce their own portion. Serve with the sliced cucumbers on the side.

Clockwise from top left: Making the chicken and stock; browning the garlic; frying the rice; Mom's magic sauce.

PRO TIP

Rendering Chicken Fat

Remove the chicken skin, slice it into ¼-inch strips and place in a pan over medium heat. When the pan is hot, the skin will begin to sizzle and release fat (reduce the heat if it seems too hot). Render until the skin is crispy, then use the released fat to make Chicken Rice or any other dish calling for oil.

Miang Kam

Savory Leaf-Bites with Tangy-Sweet Sauce

SERVES 4–6

Miang Kam is a perfect gathering dish, because each person gets to make her own custom leaf-bite. Bai chapoo, a bitter green leaf, is traditionally used for this dish, but other sturdy green leaves like collards or kale work, too. The sauce is mainly sweet and a little salty; the rest of the flavors are spicy, sour and bitter. You can get creative with additional fixings like sliced apple or jicama, if you like.

FOR THE SAUCE:

2 T. toasted coconut flakes

½ c. palm sugar

½ c. fish sauce

1 t. minced galangal

1 t. finely sliced lemongrass

2 T. ground salted shrimp

1 t. shrimp paste

FOR THE FIXINGS:

20 bai chapoo leaves (or substitute 20 3-inch x 3-inch pieces of collard or kale leaves)

½ c. diced shallots

4 fresh Thai chilies, sliced into ⅛-inch pieces

1 lime, cut into wedges

2 T. diced fresh ginger

¼ c. toasted coconut flakes

¼ c. salted dried shrimp

To make the sauce, begin by roasting ¼ cup plus 2 tablespoons of coconut flakes on a baking sheet in a 325º oven until fragrant and slightly brown. Use 2 tablespoons of the flakes for the sauce and reserve the rest for the fixings (below). Finish the sauce by combining all the ingredients in a saucepan, bring to a boil, stir to dissolve the sugar, turn off the heat and let cool.

Place the fixings in sections on a large platter surrounding a bowl of sauce with a spoon. Invite guests to build their own bites by taking a leaf, adding their preferred fixings, drizzling with the sauce and folding to eat.

CRAFT DONE LIGHT
4
FIREMANS
LIGHT

Kao Klook Kapi

Shrimp-Paste Fried Rice with Grapefruit, Chilies and Candied Pork Belly

SERVES 4

Dishes that require assembly at the table are always my first choice when throwing a dinner party, and Kao Klook Kapi is a good example. It features a showcase item—the shrimp paste-seasoned rice—and the rest is just small bites and add-ons. Although there are a lot of side ingredients, they're simple to prepare, and guests really enjoy personalizing their own bowls. The rice brings together the "five-flavor combo" (p. 27) that's so true to authentic Thai cooking.

FOR THE SIDES:

2 eggs, beaten

1 c. vegetable oil

¼ c. salted dried shrimp (found at Asian markets)

¼ c. minced grapefruit flesh

1–2 shallots, thinly sliced

3 T. thinly sliced fresh green beans

4 small green or red fresh Thai chilies, chopped into ⅛-inch pieces

½ c. Candied Pork Belly (p. 163), diced into ¼-inch pieces

Lime wedges

FOR THE RICE:

2 T. vegetable oil

2 t. minced garlic

2 T. shrimp paste

4 c. cooked, day-old jasmine rice

1 t. palm sugar

Begin making the sides by adding the eggs to a small non-stick pan and swirling them as they cook to make a thin omelet. Once cooked, roll the omelet, slice it thinly and set aside. Next, heat the oil over medium-high heat and fry the salted dried shrimp for about 1 minute. Drain the shrimp and set aside. Place the sliced omelet, fried salted shrimp, grapefruit, shallots, green beans, chilies, Candied Pork Belly and lime wedges into separate serving bowls and make the rice.

To make the rice, heat a deep pan over medium heat until hot, then add the oil. When the oil shimmers, add the garlic and fry until the garlic is brown (don't be afraid to brown garlic p. 32). Add the shrimp paste and break it into smaller pieces to mix with the oil. Add the cooked rice and palm sugar and stir and fold until the rice and shrimp paste are incorporated. Portion the rice into individual bowls and serve with the sides.

Chu Chee

Pan-Simmered Mackerel in Red Curry with Toasted Coconut Flakes and Lime Leaves

SERVES 4

I grew up near the Thai-Malaysian border. Fish is abundant there, and my grandmother often made fish curry for dinner. Chu Chee curry can be made with any type of seafood, but a meaty fish, such as mackerel or tuna, works best. Here, I've used bone-in Spanish mackerel, which you can find at local seafood markets. Some Asian grocers carry them, as well, but they're labeled Swedish Saba. If you don't have a pan big enough to fit the whole fish, cut the fish in half. For a vegetarian alternative, I really like using frozen/thawed tofu in this dish. To make the tofu, remove it from the package, drain the water and freeze the whole block on a plate. When ready to use, thaw the tofu on the counter on some paper towels. You'll be left with tofu that has a spongy texture that will absorb more flavor. If making this vegetarian, substitute the fish sauce with soy sauce.

- 2 T. coconut flakes
- 2 T. vegetable oil
- ¼ c. Red Curry Paste (p. 41)
- 1½ c. coconut cream
- 2–3 T. fish sauce
- 2 T. palm sugar
- 1–1½ lb. Spanish mackerel, cleaned and gutted
- 2 makrut lime leaves, finely julienned

Toast the coconut flakes on a small baking sheet in a 325º oven until lightly browned and set aside. Heat a large, deep pan over high heat. Turn the heat to medium-low, then add the oil and curry paste. Sauté the paste until fragrant—about 1 minute. Add the coconut cream and bring to a simmer, then add the toasted coconut flakes, fish sauce and palm sugar. Place the mackerel in the pan and let the fish simmer about 5 minutes on each side. Add the lime leaves and turn the heat off. Taste and adjust the seasoning, if needed.

SUGGESTED WINE:

OFF-DRY GERMAN RIESLING

Crab Fried Rice

SERVES 4

Growing up in the south of Thailand by the coast, we would eat fried rice, but it was always Crab Fried Rice. Generous chunks of rich crabmeat tucked throughout the rice was common, along with a few vegetables, but I always liked my fried rice with fewer veggies (or no veggies at all) so I could really enjoy the rice and meat. Give me some simple chopped green onion and eggs in my Crab Fried Rice and I'm a happy girl. This rice dish works great as a side, but it's also perfect all by itself. Just be sure to use day-old rice, as freshly made rice won't hold up to the frying. My mouth is watering just writing this recipe.

3 T. vegetable oil

2 garlic cloves, minced

Pinch salt

4 oz. crabmeat, picked over to remove any remaining shell

2 eggs

4 c. day-old cooked jasmine rice or long-grain rice (p. 37)

2 t. dark soy sauce

2 T. light soy sauce

Pinch sugar

2 T. chopped green onions

1 T. chopped cilantro, for garnish

Pinch ground white pepper, for garnish

4 whole green onions, for serving

1 cucumber, halved and sliced, for serving

Lime slices, for serving

SUGGESTED WINE:
TEXAS DRY ROSÉ

Heat a deep sauté pan (Why not a wok? p. 29) over medium heat. Add the oil and fry the garlic with the salt until fragrant and brown—about 10 seconds. Add the crabmeat and fry until slightly brown—about 30 seconds. Move the crabmeat to the side of the pan, crack in the eggs and break the yolks a bit but don't scramble all the way. Fry without stirring for 1 minute, until the eggs are cooked. Add the rice, dark soy sauce, light soy sauce and sugar and stir-fry until the rice is heated through and starts to darken—about 1 to 2 minutes. Taste and adjust seasoning. Fold in the chopped green onions and turn off the heat. Garnish with cilantro and white pepper, and serve with whole green onions, sliced cucumbers and limes.

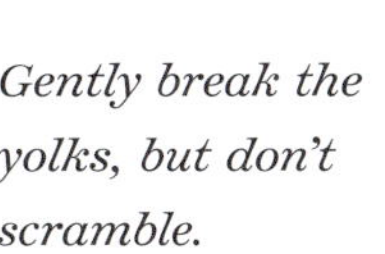

Gently break the yolks, but don't scramble.

Chicken Satay

with Creamy Peanut Sauce and Crisp Cucumber Relish

SERVES 4

We never made Chicken Satay at home; this was strictly a street-food treat and surprisingly, not that easy to find. Vendors were often hidden in corner restaurants or in alleys off the main street, but you could always follow the smoke and the distinct smell to find them. With good planning, this amazing finger food takes little time to prepare but reaps big rewards. Marinate the chicken strips a day ahead and then thread them onto the soaked skewers just before grilling. The chicken pieces, which take less than 2 minutes to grill on each side, are often served with Peanut Sauce and Cucumber Relish—another example of the complete "five-flavor combo" (p. 27) so prevalent in Thai cuisine. Traditionally, Peanut Sauce was only used to accompany Chicken Satay, but it has become so popular that it's now served as a dipping sauce for various fried foods and grilled meats.

FOR THE CHICKEN:

8 oz. boneless, skinless chicken breast or thigh meat cut into thin 4-inch x 1-inch strips

½ c. coconut milk

1 T. chopped cilantro roots or stems

2 t. curry powder

1 t. turmeric powder

2 t. sugar

2 t. fish sauce

Pinch salt

2 T. vegetable oil

12 bamboo skewers, soaked in water for 2 hours

FOR THE PEANUT SAUCE:

2 T. vegetable oil

1 T. Red Curry Paste (p. 41)

1 c. coconut milk

⅓ c. coarsely ground peanuts

2 t. sugar

½ t. salt

1 T. tamarind water, divided (p. 35)

(continued on following page)

Combine the chicken and all of the ingredients in a large bowl, mix well and marinate for at least 3 hours or, if possible, overnight. While the chicken is marinating, soak the bamboo skewers.

Heat a saucepan over medium heat and add the oil. When the oil is hot, reduce the heat to low and add the curry paste. Fry until fragrant, being careful not to burn the curry—about 15 seconds. Add the coconut milk, peanuts, sugar and salt and bring to a boil. Boil for a few minutes, or until the sauce thickens slightly. Add half the tamarind water and taste. The finished sauce should taste slightly sweet followed by a touch of tartness and saltiness. If needed, add the remaining tamarind water. Cover the pan and keep warm.

FOR THE CUCUMBER RELISH:

⅓ c. white vinegar

⅓ c. sugar

½ c. water

1 t. salt

3 pickling cucumbers, quartered and sliced ⅛-inch thick

1 thinly sliced serrano pepper

1 thinly sliced shallot

1 t. peeled, minced ginger

¼ c. chopped cilantro

SUGGESTED WINE:

SICILIAN FRAPPATO

In a medium saucepan, bring the vinegar, sugar, water and salt to a boil and stir until the sugar is dissolved. Turn off the heat and let cool. In a mixing bowl, combine the cooled liquid and the rest of the ingredients and toss well. Let the relish rest for 20 minutes.

When you're ready to grill the chicken, thread each slice onto a soaked bamboo skewer. Grill the slices over medium heat until the chicken is cooked through but still moist—about 2 minutes per side. Serve hot with the Peanut Sauce for dipping and the Cucumber Relish for bright contrast.

thaifresh

CHAPTER THREE

My Thailand

These recipes reflect a small part of the multi-layered soul of my homeland. I've travelled all over Thailand, each time discovering something new about her many regional cuisines. The country is tropical, mountainous, remote or industrialized, depending on where you land, and I love to get lost in the local culture—talking to people, seeing how they live, sampling what they grow and discovering how they've eaten for hundreds of years.

Some of these dishes were introduced to me by my mom and grandmom, and they reflect the regions where they're from; some I discovered while in college or while perusing open markets and side streets; and at least one was discovered after an eight-hour drive north from Bangkok—which I was more than happy to do. These dishes are the roadmap to my evolution as both a Thai cook and avid eater. Let me introduce you to my Thailand.

Beef Noodle Soup

with Spicy Garlic Finishing Sauce

SERVES 4

I grew up eating this soup a lot—it's my mom's favorite. In fact, she says this is the soup she craved the most when she was pregnant with me. The stock is complex from all the spices, and this is probably the only savory dish that I've seen that calls for pandan leaves (p. 31), which are usually used in desserts because of their nutty, vanilla-like flavor and fragrance. (You can find them frozen at Asian markets.) The best cut of beef to use for this dish is bone-in beef shank; it's rich in muscle and tendons, both of which are full of protein. Ask your butcher to cut the shank into thick rounds. Once the shank has simmered for a few hours, it becomes incredibly tender and offers lovely texture. The Spicy Garlic Finishing Sauce adds the perfect flavor pop.

FOR THE SPICY GARLIC FINISHING SAUCE:

2 small red or green Thai chilies, minced

2 t. fish sauce

2 garlic cloves, minced

⅓ c. white vinegar

1 t. minced cilantro stems

FOR THE SOUP:

1 t. salt

3 lb. bone-in beef shank, cut into rounds

8 c. water

2 T. dark soy sauce

¼ c. light soy sauce

2 T. sugar

5 slices galangal, cut into ⅛-inch thick slices, bruised

1 stalk lemongrass, chopped in 2-inch pieces, bruised

Handful cilantro stems

1 star anise pod

1 piece dried orange peel or 1 t. ground orange peel

2 pandan leaves

1 t. cracked black pepper

10 oz. dried rice stick, medium or large noodles

3 c. bean sprouts

½ c. chopped celery, for serving

½ c. cilantro leaves, for serving

Make the sauce by whisking all of the ingredients in a bowl. Let the mixture sit for at least 1 hour. The sauce can be made a day ahead and refrigerated.

Put the first 13 ingredients (through the black pepper) into a large stockpot and bring to a boil. Lower the heat to low and simmer for 3 hours. Meanwhile, soak the dried rice noodles in cold tap water for 1 hour. Drain and set aside with a cover to prevent the noodles from drying out. (Noodles can be soaked for several hours. You can even leave them in the water until you're ready to blanch them, if desired.) After 3 hours, remove the beef from the pot and strain the stock through a fine-mesh strainer. Put the stock back into the pot, check the seasoning and add more water, if needed. Slice the beef shank into bite-size pieces, bring the stock back to a boil and add the sliced beef back to the pot. Set up another pot of water and bring to a boil. When you're ready to serve the soup, blanch the soaked rice noodles and bean sprouts in boiling water for about 10 to 15 seconds. Add some noodles and sprouts to each bowl and ladle on some stock and beef. Top each bowl with celery, cilantro and finishing sauce.

SUGGESTED WINE:

TAVEL ROSÉ

Hor Mok

Steamed Red Curry Fish Custard

SERVES 4

This is definitely one of my grandmother's favorite dishes. She swears by using an unglazed clay bowl to do the mixing because the ingredients get moved around over a rough surface, thus creating a thicker mixture. Not everyone has an unglazed clay bowl handy though, so a ceramic bowl or stainless-steel bowl will work. Traditionally, this dish is cooked in individual, handmade banana-leaf bowls in a big steamer, but not everyone has those available, either. I've found that using ramekins and a water-bath method in the oven produces a similar result. If you have a steamer that will fit four ramekins in it, then by all means, use it! Just remember the mixture will set faster in a steamer.

1½ c. coconut cream, divided

¼ c. Red Curry Paste (p. 41)

1 lb. red snapper, cut into 1½-inch cubes

1 egg

1 T. fish sauce

1 T. rice flour

3 T. julienned makrut lime leaves

1 c. chopped cabbage, white or green (2-inch pieces)

1 c. Thai basil leaves

Sliced red pepper, for garnish

Makrut lime leaves, for garnish

Cilantro, for garnish

Fish sauce, for serving

Thai Chilies in Fish Sauce condiment (p. 161), for serving

Heat the oven to 350º. Heat a pan or kettle of water on the stove. In a large bowl, combine ¾ cup of the coconut cream and the curry paste and mix until blended. Add the fish pieces and stir slowly in a consistent motion—almost like you're making mayonnaise—until the mixture is thickened. Add the egg, fish sauce, the remainder of the coconut cream minus 2 tablespoons (reserve for garnish) and the rice flour and stir to combine. Line 4 8-oz. oven-proof ramekins with the cabbage and Thai basil. Portion the fish mixture into the ramekins. Place the ramekins into a deep-sided baking pan and fill the pan with the hot water to halfway up the sides of the ramekins. Carefully place the pan in the oven and bake for 1 hour. Check after 1 hour; if the mixture isn't set (almost like a thick paste), continue to bake until set and the fish cooked. Garnish with the reserved coconut cream, sliced red pepper, lime leaves and cilantro. Let cool for 15 minutes before serving. Serve with a side of fish sauce and the Thai Chilies in Fish Sauce condiment.

15-Minute Green Curry Fried Rice

SERVES 4

This is a quick dish using both leftover Green Curry with Sirloin and Summer Squash (p. 53) and cooked jasmine rice (p. 37)—a yummy dinner in 15 minutes! When you stir-fry the leftover curry and rice together in a hot dry pan, the blast of heat gives the dish a different flavor than simply folding the two together. Of course, if you wanted to make the curry from scratch, simply follow the Green Curry with Sirloin and Summer Squash recipe up to adding the veggies, and simmer it a little longer to thicken. You'll still need to use day-old cooked rice, though, because freshly cooked rice won't hold up as well when frying. You can add veggies of your choice at the very end if you like.

1 c. leftover Green Curry with Sirloin and Summer Squash

3 c. leftover cooked jasmine rice

1 T. fish sauce, more if needed

½ c. Thai basil leaves

Thai Chilies and Fish Sauce condiment (p. 161), for serving

Heat a deep pan over medium-high heat. When the pan is very hot, add the curry and bring to a boil. Lower the heat to simmer and let the curry cook for a minute to thicken. Add the leftover rice and stir-fry until the curry and rice are thoroughly mixed. Season with fish sauce and fold in the Thai basil. If making the curry from scratch, add the veggies of your choice at this time and fold in. Cook for a few minutes to let the veggies soften. Serve the fried rice with the Thai Chilies and Fish Sauce condiment.

Yellow Curry with Shrimp and Potato

SERVES 4

Yellow curry is of Indian origin. It's mild, but still has enough spice to satisfy those who like a little heat while considering the rest of the palates at the table. This recipe is a customer favorite and a special request for this book. Be sure to use large shrimp; they work best with this particular curry.

- 2 13½-oz. unshaken cans of coconut milk
- ½ c. Yellow Curry Paste (p. 41)
- 2 lb. large shrimp, shelled, deveined
- 4 c. 1½-inch potato cubes (Yukon Gold or new potatoes work best)
- 1 medium onion, chopped into bite-size pieces
- 3–4 T. fish sauce
- 1 T. palm sugar
- Cooked white rice, for serving

Scoop out the cream from the top half of each can of coconut milk and place into a medium saucepan. (Make sure to scoop all the way to halfway or you won't have enough coconut cream to work with.) Bring the coconut cream to a boil over medium heat and boil for one minute. Add the curry paste and stir to mix until smooth with no lumps. Adjust the heat to simmer and cook—without stirring—until the mixture is fragrant and the coconut cream starts to release some oil, about 3 to 5 minutes. (You'll start to see yellow oil on the surface.) Add the shrimp, stir and cook for 1 minute. Remove the shrimp to a plate and set aside. Add the rest of the coconut milk to the pot and bring to a boil. Add the potatoes and onions and let simmer for another 10 minutes. Add the fish sauce and palm sugar, then return the shrimp to the pot. Stir to combine. Adjust the seasoning, to taste. Turn off the heat and serve with rice.

Crispy Chicken Cracklings

MAKES ABOUT 50 CRACKLINGS

One of our all-time favorite snacks as kids was Crispy Chicken Cracklings. My mom would fry the pieces, then let them drain on paper towels for us to circle around and snatch. Chicken cracklings are thinner and more fragrant than pork cracklings, and they're so easy to make. Use the skin from chicken pieces purchased at the market or ask your butcher if they sell just the skin. Eat the cracklings plain with a splash of Homemade Sriracha Sauce (p. 159), as a crunchy topping for noodles or soups or eat them as larb (recipe below).

- 2 lb. chicken skin, cut into 1-inch x 2-inch pieces
- 3 T. light soy sauce
- 1 t. ground white pepper
- ½ c. all-purpose flour (or rice flour, for a gluten-free version)
- 4 c. vegetable oil

Marinate the chicken skin pieces in the soy sauce and white pepper for 1 hour. Once marinated, drain the liquid (if any), toss the pieces in the flour and turn to coat. In a medium pot, heat the oil to 350º. Sprinkle in half of the pieces and fry until crispy, golden and beginning to float to the surface. Use a slotted spoon or kitchen spider to remove to paper towels, then fry the other half.

Crispy Chicken-Crackling Larb with Sticky Rice

SERVES 2

- 3 T. lime juice
- ¼ t. Roasted Thai Chili Flakes (p. 161)
- 1–2 T. fish or soy sauce
- 2 shallots, thinly sliced
- ¼ c. mixed mint and cilantro leaves
- 2 T. chopped green onions, white and green parts
- 2 T. Toasted Ground Sticky Rice (p. 155)
- 25 Crispy Chicken Cracklings
- Cooked sticky rice (p. 39), for eating

Combine all of the ingredients except the cracklings and cooked sticky rice and toss to combine. Add the cracklings and mix. Serve with sticky rice for eating by hand.

Kai Kata

Pan Eggs with Pork and Chicken Sausage

SERVES 1

On a trip home to Thailand in 2017, I heard about Kai Kata—literally, "pan eggs." Everyone told me I needed to try this dish. Walking down the street one morning to the market in Chiang Mai, I noticed a vendor selling it and I had to stop. The dish arrived at the table looking humble, but it was one of the best breakfasts I could have asked for. Everything is cooked and served in a personal pan, so if you have those little individual cast-iron pans, those work best. If not, use a small skillet. Hot or mild Italian sausage or diced ham can be used in place of the ground pork. Here, I've added applewood-smoked chicken sausage because I think the sweetness brightens the dish.

3 oz. ground pork
½ t. minced garlic
¼ t. ground cumin
¼ t. freshly ground black pepper
1 t. light soy sauce
2 T. vegetable oil
1 link applewood-smoked chicken sausage, sliced ¼-inch thick
2 eggs
2 T. chopped green onions
1 T. chopped cilantro
Small bunch, microgreens, for serving
Pinch black or white pepper, for serving
Hot sauce of your choice, for serving

SUGGESTED WINE:
SPARKLING WINE

In a mixing bowl, combine the ground pork, garlic, cumin, black pepper and soy sauce and mix well. Heat the oil in a personal cast-iron or small frying pan. Add the ground pork mixture and sauté—breaking up the meat as it cooks. Push the pork to the side of the pan, add the sliced sausage and sauté. Move the sausage to the side of the pan and crack in the eggs. When the eggs are cooked to your desired doneness, add the green onions and cilantro and turn off the heat. Top with microgreens and a pinch of pepper and serve with the hot sauce of your choice.

Kang Om Curry with Pork Ribs

Northern-Style Stock-Based Curry

SERVES 4

This is another dish I fell in love with while visiting Northern Thailand. There are no coconut plantations in that part of the country, so most of the northern curries are stock-based and soupier. This curry paste is easy to make with few ingredients, and the vegetables are available at most markets.

FOR THE CURRY PASTE:

6 small dried red Thai chilies, fried, divided

1 shallot, diced

1 garlic clove, minced

¼ t. salt

1 stalk lemongrass, tough outer layer removed, thinly sliced

2 ⅛-inch slices galangal, diced

3 makrut lime leaves, thinly sliced

FOR THE CURRY:

2 T. vegetable oil

1 recipe curry paste

4 c. water

2½ lb. pork ribs, cut into individual ribs and then cut into 2-inch segments (ask your butcher)

2–4 T. fish sauce

1 c. unpeeled, 1-inch acorn or delicata squash cubes

½ c. chopped green beans, about 1½-inch pieces

½ c. oyster mushroom pieces

½ c. sliced zucchini

½ c. chopped dill

2 T. Toasted Ground Sticky Rice (p. 155)

3 remaining fried dried Thai chilies

½ c. Thai basil leaves

2 green onions, green and white parts, chopped into 1½-inch pieces

Sticky rice, for serving (p. 39)

To make the paste, fry the 6 dried chilies in a small pan with a splash of vegetable oil until fragrant and darker in color, then set aside. Using a large mortar and pestle, pound together the shallot, garlic, 3 of the fried chilies (reserve the rest for the curry below), salt, lemongrass, galangal and lime leaves until a paste is formed.

Finish the curry by heating a large pot over medium heat. Add the oil, then turn the heat to low. Add the paste and sauté until fragrant—about 10 to 15 seconds. Add the water to the pot and bring to a boil. Lower the heat to simmer, add the ribs and fish sauce and simmer for another 45 minutes to an hour. Add the squash cubes and cook for 3 minutes. Add the green beans, mushrooms and zucchini and simmer for about 2 more minutes. Add the dill, ground sticky rice, the reserved fried chilies and the Thai basil and stir. Fold in the green onions and serve with sticky rice or jasmine rice.

Pad Prik King

Stir-Fried Red Curry with Crispy Pork Belly and Green Beans

SERVES 4

My mom taught me how to make her version of Pad Prik King. She likes her food a bit on the sweet side, so adjust the palm sugar to your taste (though I think this version is delicious). You can make this dish with just the Crispy Pork Belly (p. 164), or you can add green beans like Mom's version.

2 T. vegetable oil

3 T. Red Curry Paste (p. 41)

1 c. chopped Crispy Pork Belly (½-inch thick pieces)

3 c. sliced green beans (1 ½-inch pieces sliced at an angle)

⅓ c. water, divided

1–2 t. fish sauce

2 T. (or more) palm sugar

1 T. thinly julienned makrut lime leaves

Cooked jasmine rice (p. 37), for serving

Heat a sauté pan to medium, then adjust the heat to low. Add the oil and curry paste and fry until fragrant—about 30 seconds. Add the pork belly pieces and sauté for about 1 to 2 minutes. Add the green beans and continue to cook until the beans soften, adding water—about 2 tablespoons at a time—to moisten the mixture and help the beans steam. (The beans are done when they turn bright green.) Season with fish sauce and palm sugar—adding a little water, if necessary, to create a little sauce. Add the lime leaves and fold everything together. Serve over jasmine rice.

SUGGESTED WINE:

ITALIAN FIANO

Koong Ob Woon Sen

Clay Pot Shrimp, Pork and Bean Thread Noodles

SERVES 4

I'm always drawn to any vendor making Koong Ob Woon Sen—an intoxicating shrimp, pork and bean thread noodle dish cooked in a clay pot. The lure of the herbs and spices promises that this dish will not only satisfy your hunger, but cure what ails you. It's the heady smell of pork belly sizzling at the bottom of the clay pot blending with the fresh grassy scent of the cilantro roots and the bright pop of ginger that makes this dish so irresistibly fragrant. For the best results, use an ovenproof clay pot, but a small Dutch oven will also work.

2 T. vegetable oil

2 cilantro roots or 10 cilantro stems, bruised by smashing with the side of a knife

3 ¼-inch rounds fresh ginger, unpeeled

½ t. salt

1 small onion, thinly sliced

1 T. crushed whole black peppercorns (use a plastic bag and a rolling pin or skillet to crush)

6 oz. bean thread (glass) noodles, soaked 20 minutes in room-temperature water

3 T. light soy sauce

1 T. whiskey (optional, but traditional)

1 T. sugar

1 T. sesame oil

1 lb. large shrimp, heads/shells on, washed thoroughly

3 slices bacon or ¼ c. pork belly chunks

Chopped green onions, for garnish

Heat the oven to 350º. Then heat a wok or deep sauté pan over medium heat and add the vegetable oil. When the oil is hot, add the cilantro roots or stems, ginger, salt, onion and peppercorns and stir-fry until fragrant—about 10 to 15 seconds. Remove the mixture to a large mixing bowl and add the soaked bean thread noodles, light soy sauce, whiskey (if using), sugar, sesame oil and shrimp and mix well with a spoon. Lay the bacon or pork belly on the bottom of the clay pot or Dutch oven and pour the mixture on top. Top with the lid or foil and bake for 20 minutes. After 20 minutes, check to see if the shrimp are cooked (they should be pink all the way through). If they are still opaque, let them cook a little longer. Add the green onions, cover, and let the onions steam in the oven for another 30 seconds. Remove from the oven and serve.

Kao Soi

Northern-Style Egg Noodle Curry

SERVES 4

I grew up in the southern part of Thailand where beaches were my backyard. But after college graduation, I got to explore the mountains and the northern parts of Thailand more—especially the food. I fell in love with this noodle curry in Chiang Mai, and I would happily drive eight hours just to eat it. I now keep a running list of the places serving the best Kao Soi, and I visit a few every trip. Using fresh egg noodles is important to achieve the most authentic texture and flavor, though other fresh noodles can be substituted (I have to use rice noodles because of my allergy to wheat, and it's still delicious). This dish is a true blend of Thai, Indian and Burmese—a perfect example of the neighboring influences found in Thai cuisine. Interestingly, the flavors also remind me of southern Thai food, and that's maybe why I love it so much. It tastes like home.

FOR THE CURRY PASTE:

4 dried long red Thai or Hatch chilies

3 T. chopped shallots

1 T. chopped garlic

1 T. chopped fresh turmeric root, unpeeled

2 T. chopped fresh ginger

1 t. salt

2 t. minced cilantro stems

FOR THE FRIED SHALLOT GARNISH:

¼ lb. thinly sliced shallots

⅛ t. salt

2 c. vegetable oil

(continued on following page)

Make the paste by toasting the chilies, shallots, garlic, turmeric root and ginger—1 at a time—in a dry pan over low heat for 1 to 2 minutes each. Allow to cool, then use a large mortar and pestle to pound the ingredients together with the salt and cilantro stems until smooth. A blender can be substituted.

For the garnish, combine the shallots and salt in a bowl and mix. Heat the oil in a deep pot over medium heat. Add the shallots and fry until golden and crispy, about 5 to 7 minutes. Remove to a paper towel-lined plate to drain. Once cooled completely, either use immediately or store in an airtight container in the refrigerator for up to 1 month. Makes about 2 cups.

FOR THE NOODLES:

1 13½-oz. unshaken can coconut milk (if the can has been shaken, let it sit in the fridge overnight or on the shelf for 4 to 5 days)

6 oz. chicken breast or thigh meat, sliced very thinly

1 T. palm sugar

2 T. light soy sauce

1½ c. Chicken Stock (p. 150)

1 c. fresh egg noodles

1 T. chopped green onions, for garnish

1 T. chopped cilantro, for garnish

Lime wedges, for garnish

2 T. fried shallots, for garnish

½ t. Fried Thai Chilies condiment (p. 168), for garnish

¼ c. Pickled Chinese Cabbage (p. 166), for garnish

SUGGESTED WINE:

FRENCH GAMAY

Heat a frying pan over low heat. Using a spoon, scoop out only the creamy top half of the unshaken can of coconut milk and add it to the pan. Simmer the coconut cream until it's thick and shiny on the surface—about 2 minutes. Add the curry paste, mix well and let simmer, without stirring, at low heat until fragrant—about 4 minutes. Add the chicken slices and simmer until the chicken is just cooked on the outside. Season with the palm sugar and soy sauce, then add the stock and continue to simmer until the chicken is cooked through—about 5 minutes (add more stock or water, if needed). Blanch the fresh egg noodles in boiling water for about 15 seconds, then drain and place in a large bowl. Ladle the chicken curry on top and serve with the green onions, cilantro, lime wedges, fried shallots, Fried Thai Chilis condiment and Pickled Chinese Cabbage.

Fresh turmeric root at the market.

โล 40

Tom Kha

Coconut Soup with Exotic Mushrooms, Shrimp and Salty-Sour Finishing Sauce

SERVES 4–6

Tom Kha wasn't a regular on our table growing up, but I remember my mom making it here and there with different kinds of produce, like fresh bamboo shoots or fresh banana blossoms. It wasn't until I moved to the U.S. that I realized how unbelievably popular this soup is—and for good reason. Coconut milk gives the soup a velvety texture, and there's a perfect balance of salty, sweet, spicy, sour and bitter flavors. It's easily one of the most ordered dishes at Thai Fresh. This recipe is tried and true; my dad says it's the best coconut soup he's ever had—and he's not usually one to compliment.

FOR THE FINISHING SAUCE:

3 T. fish sauce or 2½ T. light soy sauce (add ¼ t. sugar if using light soy sauce)

4 T. lime juice

½ t. minced small fresh Thai chilies (or more for a spicier soup)

1 T. cilantro leaves

FOR THE SOUP:

1 13½-oz. can coconut milk

2 c. chicken or vegetable stock

6 ⅛-inch slices galangal, bruised with the back of a knife

1 stalk lemongrass, tough outer layers removed, bruised with the back of a knife, then cut into 1½-inch pieces

1 small fresh Thai chili, smashed with the side of a knife

1 shallot, cut in half, smashed with the side of a knife

3 makrut lime leaves, torn into small pieces

1 t. palm or white sugar

¼ t. salt

4 c. mixed exotic mushrooms (shiitake, oyster, chanterelle, enoki, etc.), torn or sliced into bite-size pieces

1½ c. peeled shrimp

To make the sauce, mix everything together in a small bowl and set aside.

To make the soup, combine the coconut milk and stock in a large pot and bring to a boil. Reduce the heat to low, add everything but the mushrooms and simmer for a couple of minutes. Add the mushrooms and shrimp and continue simmering until the mushrooms are tender, about 4 to 5 minutes. Turn off the heat and top with the finishing sauce. Before serving, remove the galangal and lemongrass pieces (or instruct guests to eat around them). Serve as an appetizer or as an entrée with rice.

CHAPTER FOUR

Glorious Street Food

Street food is a way of life in Thailand. We'd venture out to the markets in the morning to get fresh produce for dinner, and along the way, grab something for a walkable breakfast. If we stayed out long enough, lunch was a bowl of hot fragrant noodles, crunchy fried chicken or a bright salad of shredded green papaya from our favorite vendor.

In Thailand, street-food vendors set up near one another and become a community of sorts. They often sell complementary dishes next to each other, so you can get a favorite dish from one stall, and another from the neighboring stall—like an informal cafeteria.

These recipes are my love letter to Thai street food. They're the foods I seek out time and again when I'm in Thailand, and ones I make in my Austin home when I get a craving. Let me share the streets of Thailand with you.

Kanom Jeen Nam Ya

Noodles with Fish Curry

SERVES 8

In Thailand, there are several variations of Kanom Jeen Nam Ya, a fresh noodle dish with fish. The handmade noodles are purchased at the market, then topped with different types of curries. For this recipe, I use dried angel-hair pasta or dried Vietnamese rice noodles, which have a very similar texture to the fresh noodles once cooked.

6 c. water, divided

1½ lb. red snapper, cut into 2-inch pieces

15 long dried red Thai chilies, stemmed, seeded, soaked in water for 20 minutes, chopped

1 c. roughly chopped shallots

1 c. whole garlic cloves

2 c. finely minced wild ginger (found in Asian markets—also known as "lesser galangal" or "krachai")

3 makrut limes leaves, torn

1 T. finely minced galangal

3 T. thinly sliced lemongrass

1 t. shrimp paste

6 oz. salted fish (found packed in oil at Asian markets; dry, salted cod works, too)

1 lb. dried angel-hair pasta or dried Vietnamese rice noodles

10 small dried red Thai chilies, fried, for serving

2 13½-oz. unshaken cans coconut milk

¼–½ c. fish sauce

2 t. salt

FOR SERVING:

1 c. thinly sliced raw green beans

1 c. quartered and sliced cucumbers

1 c. bean sprouts

1 c. Thai basil or lemon basil

1 c. Pickled Chinese Cabbage (p. 166)

1 c. sliced hearts of palm in water

1 c. thinly sliced purple cabbage

6 hard-boiled eggs

Fried chilies

Bring 2 cups of the water to a boil in a medium saucepan. Add the fish pieces and cook for 3 minutes. Strain out the snapper—reserving the water—and adjust the heat to medium-low. Set the fish aside to cool. Once cool, break the fish into very small pieces. Meanwhile, add the chilies, shallots, garlic, wild ginger, lime leaves, galangal, lemongrass and shrimp paste to the reserved cooking water in the pan. Add a bit more water, if needed—the mixture should look like a saucy paste but not soupy. Remove from the heat and blend the mixture in a blender along with the salted fish until combined (add a little more water if you think the mixture is too thick to blend). Add the snapper and set aside.

Bring another pot of water to a boil and cook the angel-hair pasta or Vietnamese rice noodles until al dente. If using rice noodles, transfer them to an ice bath once cooked. While the noodles cook, fry the dried chilies in a small skillet with a splash of oil until fragrant and darker in color, then set aside.

Scoop out the creamy top half of the unshaken cans of coconut milk, place into a bowl and set aside. Pour the rest of the coconut milk from the cans into a deep pot and add the remaining 4 cups of water. Bring to a boil and let simmer for 1 to 2 minutes. Add the fish mixture and stir to combine. Let the mixture simmer for 3 to 5 minutes (there should be a little bit of red oil that rises to the surface). Stir in the fish sauce, salt and the reserved coconut cream, bring to a boil and turn off the heat. Place the noodles on a large platter and top with the fish curry. Serve the veggies, herbs, eggs and fried chilies on the side.

Grilled Pork Skewers

with Spicy Lime Sauce

SERVES 4

This is probably my favorite street-food snack; the sweet smell of palm sugar and soy sauce always draws me in. Whenever I go back to Thailand, my brother goes out early in the morning to grab an order for my first breakfast home.

FOR THE PORK AND MARINADE:

1 lb. pork butt or shoulder, sliced into 2-inch x 4-inch pieces, about ½-inch thick

¼ c. light soy sauce

1 T. palm sugar

1 t. salt

2 T. vegetable oil

1 T. minced cilantro stems

1 t. black pepper

4 cloves garlic, minced

Bamboo skewers, soaked in water for 2 hours

FOR THE SPICY LIME SAUCE:

3 T. lime juice

2 T. fish sauce

1 t. sugar

¼ t. (or more) Roasted Thai Chili Flakes (p. 161)

1 shallot, sliced thinly

1 T. chopped cilantro

SUGGESTED WINE:

UNOAKED CHARDONNAY

In a large bowl, mix together all of the marinade ingredients. Add the pork pieces and marinate in the refrigerator for at least 3 hours or overnight.

Mix together all of the sauce ingredients and set aside. When the pork has finished marinating, thread the pieces on the soaked skewers and grill for about 3 minutes per side. Serve with the sauce and side of sticky rice (p. 39).

Kao Ka Moo

Brothy Pork and Rice with Spicy Garlic Sauce, Blanched Broccoli and Pickled Chinese Cabbage

SERVES 8

Kao Ka Moo is a brothy street-food delicacy made with bone-in, skin-on pork leg. The skin becomes tender and adds so much flavor to the stock. Some of the most popular Kao Ka Moo stall vendors keep their big pots of broth simmering all day and night, and just keep adding to the broth as necessary. Served with a Spicy Garlic Sauce, blanched broccoli and Pickled Chinese Cabbage (p. 166), this is a perfect Thai dish for a celebration or holiday. The aroma of the spices that have been simmered all day will welcome happy, hungry guests.

FOR THE SPICY GARLIC SAUCE:

2 small red or green fresh Thai chilies, minced

2 t. fish sauce

2 garlic cloves, minced

⅓ c. white vinegar

1 t. minced cilantro stems

FOR THE PORK AND BROTH:

3–4 lb. bone-in, skin-on pork leg or shoulder

6–8 c. water

4 garlic cloves, mashed

3 cilantro roots, or 6 cilantro stems

1 T. cracked black pepper

2 whole star anise pods

2 cinnamon sticks

4 T. dark soy sauce

¼ c. light soy sauce

¼ c. fish sauce

⅓ c. palm sugar

FOR SERVING:

Cooked jasmine rice (p. 37)

4 c. chopped broccoli, blanched

Pickled Chinese Cabbage (p. 166)

SUGGESTED WINE:

AUSTRALIAN GRENACHE

Make the sauce by combining all the ingredients in a bowl. Let the mixture sit for at least 1 hour. The sauce can be made a day ahead and refrigerated.

For the pork and broth, add all of the ingredients to a big pot and bring to a boil. Reduce the heat to low and simmer for 4 to 6 hours. Then remove the pork to cool and strain the broth through a fine-mesh strainer—reserving the broth but discarding the solids. Keep the broth warm. Meanwhile, blanch the chopped broccoli in boiling water for about 3 minutes. Cut the pork into bite-size pieces and serve it, along with a little broth, over cooked jasmine rice. Top with the Spicy Garlic Sauce, broccoli and Pickled Chinese Cabbage.

Pad Ka Prow

Holy Basil Pork

SERVES 4

This is a school cafeteria favorite, but don't let that fool you into thinking this is bland, packaged fare. School cafeterias in Thailand are nothing like the ones here in the U.S. There are vendors lined up to sell the best foods you can find locally, and as kids, we always looked forward to getting to eat at school. Trays and trays of freshly prepared food greeted you in the morning as you arrived, and you just picked what you wanted to eat to start your day. American-style "breakfast food" is not a thing in Thailand. We ate soups, curries and this spicy stir-fry. I always ordered a fried egg on mine, so that's what I offer below. You can modify this dish by using less meat and adding vegetables like green beans, mushrooms or onions. Watch the spice level on this one. If you like it hot, go heavy on the Thai peppers. It's a dish I started to add more spice to as I got older.

2 garlic cloves

Pinch salt

1 T. chopped shallot

2–4 fresh Thai chilies, to taste

2 T. vegetable oil

8 oz. ground pork

1–2 T. fish sauce

Pinch sugar

1 c. holy basil leaves (or substitute Thai basil leaves)

Cooked jasmine rice (p. 37), for serving

Fried egg, for topping

SUGGESTED WINE:

SPARKLING ROSÉ

Make a paste by pounding together the garlic, salt, shallot and chilies using a mortar and pestle. Alternatively, you can mince all the ingredients by hand and combine. Heat a wok or a deep sauté pan over medium-high heat. When hot, turn down the heat a little, add the oil and fry the paste for about 20 seconds. Add the pork and continue to stir-fry for a few minutes. Add the fish sauce and sugar, taste, then adjust the seasonings, if necessary. Add the holy basil leaves and stir-fry until the basil is soft—about 20 seconds. Remove from the heat, serve over jasmine rice and top with a fried egg.

Fried Chicken

SERVES 4

Vendors selling fried chicken are everywhere on the streets of Thailand—usually near the vendors selling Papaya Salad (p. 125), and Larb (p. 116), because they're best eaten together. This recipe features a lighter batter that won't make you feel like taking a nap after eating it. If you have a deep fryer, you can use that, otherwise a large pot or Dutch oven works. The marinated chicken can also be grilled without the flour. If grilling, I like the chicken a little bit sweeter, so I double the amount of palm sugar to get that caramelized flavor.

1 T. white peppercorns

2 T. minced garlic

1 t. salt

2 T. minced cilantro roots or stems

⅓ c. light soy sauce

2 t. palm sugar

1 small whole chicken (about 3 lb.), broken down into smaller pieces (or simply buy drumsticks, bone-in thighs and split breasts to save the work; you'll need to cut the split breasts into 3 pieces each)

6 c. vegetable oil

2 c. rice flour

Using a mortar and pestle, pound together the peppercorns, garlic, salt and cilantro roots or stems into a paste. Add the soy sauce and palm sugar to the paste and rub the mixture all over the chicken pieces. Marinate for at least 6 hours in the refrigerator. When the chicken has marinated, heat the oil in a large Dutch oven or pot to 350º. Dredge the chicken pieces in the flour and shake off the excess. Using tongs, carefully add the chicken to the hot oil in batches of 4 pieces. Fry each batch until golden and starting to float to the top of the oil—about 10 minutes. Remove each batch to a platter lined with paper towels to drain. Serve hot.

Kao Mok Pae

Muslim-Style Rice with Goat and Sweet Chili Sauce

SERVES 6

I have a true love for the Muslim-style rice dish, Kao Mok Pae, and growing up in a Muslim community, we had access to it all the time. My mom is from Central Thailand and she fell in love with this dish when she moved south to be with my dad. For those familiar with the Indian dish biryani, you'll see the influences here. We used to eat it every week, yet we never made it at home. This was a destination treat for our family, and our favorite vendor would always sell out before 2 p.m. Kao Mok Pae is usually made with chicken, but the recipe I've included uses goat meat. The rice and the goat together are uniquely aromatic, and the fried shallots add the perfect finishing texture. This is another wonderful dish for a gathering.

FOR THE GOAT AND MARINATING PASTE:

1½ lb. goat meat, stew cut

1 t. coriander seeds

2 t. cumin seeds

2 cloves

1-inch piece cassia bark or cinnamon stick

1½ T. chopped fresh turmeric root (preferred), or ½ t. dried turmeric

1½ T. minced garlic

2 T. chopped ginger

2 t. salt

FOR THE SWEET CHILI SAUCE:

2 long fresh red Thai chilies (or substitute red serrano peppers), seeded, minced

1–2 small fresh Thai chilies, minced

2 cilantro roots or 5 cilantro stems, minced

Large pinch salt

1 large garlic clove, minced

⅓ c. white sugar

⅓ c. white vinegar

(continued on following page)

Make the marinating paste first by heating a dry frying pan over medium-low heat. Add the coriander seeds to the pan and move them around constantly until fragrant and lightly browned—about 1 to 2 minutes. Remove to a small bowl. Next, add the cumin seeds to the pan and heat until fragrant and lightly browned. Add them to a separate small bowl and set aside (the coriander and cumin seeds need to be toasted separately because they toast at different rates). After the seeds are finished, add the cloves and the cassia bark (or cinnamon stick) to the pan and toast until fragrant. Adding 1 at a time, pound together the seeds, cloves, cassia bark, turmeric, garlic, ginger and salt using a mortar and pestle. If you don't have a mortar and pestle, grind the dried spices together in a coffee grinder or crush in a plastic bag using a heavy skillet, then transfer to a blender, add the fresh ingredients and blend until smooth. Rub the marinating paste all over the goat pieces, place in a large plastic bag and transfer to the fridge for 3 to 5 hours.

To make the sauce, combine all the ingredients in a frying pan and bring to a simmer over medium heat until a thick syrup is formed—about 5 minutes. Let the sauce cool before serving.

FOR THE RICE:

I piece cassia bark or cinnamon stick

2–3 Thai or Indian cardamom pods (if using Indian cardamom, use the white or gray ones, not the green ones, which are too pungent)

3 c. vegetable oil for deep-frying

5 shallots, sliced

Marinated goat meat

2 t. salt

4 c. uncooked long-grain white rice (long-grain rice is better than jasmine rice in this recipe because jasmine rice has more moisture and tends to become too mushy after it's cooked with marinated meat)

6 c. Chicken Stock (p. 150)

2 bay leaves

SUGGESTED WINE:

ITALIAN NEBBIOLO

Toast the cassia bark or cinnamon stick and the cardamom pods in a small, dry skillet using the method above, then set aside. When the goat has finished marinating, remove it from the fridge. Heat the oil in a large, deep-frying pan over medium heat to 350º. When hot, add the shallots and deep-fry until golden—about 4 minutes, stirring occasionally. Remove the shallots to a paper towel, then add the goat pieces to the oil. Fry the goat for about 3 minutes on each side, then remove to a plate. Carefully remove and discard all but ¼ cup of the frying oil from the pan, then add all but ¼ cup of the shallots (reserve for garnish), the fried goat meat, the salt, rice, stock, cassia bark, cardamom pods and finally, the bay leaves, and bring to a boil. Turn down the heat to very low and cover the pot. When the rice is cooked—about 15 to 20 minutes—the goat should also be done. If the rice is not yet done, stir to rotate from top to bottom, sprinkle on a little water—about ¼ cup—and let cook at very low heat for another 5 minutes. Remove from the heat and transfer to a serving dish. Top with the reserved fried shallots and serve with the sweet chili sauce.

Mushroom Larb

Mushroom Salad Wrap

SERVES 8

Most of the time, you'll see larb made with ground pork or meat. Sometimes, I like making it with less meat, and have found that adding different types of exotic mushrooms is a good way to get that meaty texture without all the meat. Many farmers markets will often have one or two exotic mushroom vendors; explore and try different types of mushrooms to see what you like best. Larb is most often served in a lettuce wrap as a "salad."

¼ c. Chicken Stock (p. 150) or vegetable stock

1 t. white sugar

¼ t. salt

1 t. minced garlic

8 oz. mixed mushrooms (shiitake, oyster, chanterelle, pioppini, king trumpet, etc.), wiped clean and cut into small pieces

3 T. lime juice

¼ t. Roasted Thai Chili Flakes (p. 161)

1–2 T. fish sauce or soy sauce

2 thinly sliced shallots

¼ c. mixed mint and cilantro leaves

2 T. Toasted Ground Sticky Rice (p. 155)

Cabbage, bibb or green leaf lettuce leaves, for serving

Heat the stock, sugar and salt in a sauté pan over medium-high heat. Add the garlic and mushrooms and sauté until cooked—about 3 to 4 minutes. Season with lime juice, Roasted Thai Chili Flakes and fish sauce or soy sauce. Mix in the shallots, herbs and Toasted Ground Sticky Rice. Taste and adjust the seasoning, as needed. Serve on a platter with a side of cabbage leaves, bibb lettuce leaves or green leaf lettuce to make wraps.

Rice Congee with Pork

SERVES 4

Rice Congee, a type of porridge, is an early morning and late-night treat that's usually purchased from a Thai street vendor. (We never made it at home although it's easy to make.) During my college years, there was a popular Rice Congee stall right across the street from the university. I remember many mornings waiting in line for my bowl. Plain congee (the first 4 ingredients below) can be frozen for up to a year.

1 c. broken jasmine rice (available at Asian markets, or make your own by placing the rice in a food processor and pulsing until it's broken but not ground)

6 c. water

1 t. plus 1 pinch salt, divided

1 pandan leaf

6 oz. ground pork

4 T. light soy sauce, divided

2 c. Chicken Stock (p. 150)

2 eggs

2–4 T. finely shredded ginger

1 T. chopped green onions

Pinch ground white pepper

Place the broken rice in a medium bowl, cover with tap water and soak for 1 hour. Drain and set aside. Bring 6 cups of water to a boil in a large saucepan, add 1 teaspoon of the salt and the pandan leaf. Add the soaked rice, reduce the heat to low and cook for 30 to 45 minutes—stirring occasionally to prevent the rice from sticking to the bottom of the pan. In a bowl, mix together the pork, pinch of salt and 1 tablespoon of the soy sauce. Add the stock to the rice and bring to a boil. Pinch the pork mixture into small clumps and add to the simmering congee. Let the mixture cook for a few minutes over medium-low heat until the pork is cooked, about 4 to 5 minutes—adding more stock or water, if needed. Add the remaining 3 tablespoons of soy sauce, taste and adjust with salt, if needed. Turn off the heat, remove and discard the pandan leaf, gently crack in the eggs and let the congee sit, undisturbed, for a few minutes to let the eggs set. Sprinkle on the ginger, green onions and white pepper and serve.

Pad Thai

SERVES 2

In Thailand, my family never made Pad Thai at home—this was strictly a street food, and often a long line awaited us at the most popular stalls. Interestingly, Pad Thai is relatively new to Thailand—it's only about 75 years old. Originally, tofu was the protein of choice, but the recipe has changed over the years to include pork or shrimp. The sauce can be made ahead of time and kept for several months in the fridge (or indefinitely in the freezer), so make a big batch to enjoy later!

6 oz. dried rice stick noodles

2 T. crushed roasted peanuts, for topping

2 T. palm sugar

1 T. white sugar

2 T. tamarind water (p. 35)

2 T. fish sauce

3 T. vegetable oil, divided

2 t. minced shallot

8 medium shrimp, peeled, deveined

2 eggs

½ c. fried tofu (p. 44), cut into ¼-inch pieces

Pinch Roasted Thai Chili Flakes (p. 161)

2 t. minced dried salted shrimp (available at Asian markets and online)

1 t. salted radish (available at Asian markets and online)

2 c. bean sprouts, divided

1 c. sliced Chinese chives, also called garlic chives (Chinese chives are available at Asian markets) or scallions (green parts only), cut into 2-inch pieces, divided

Lime wedges, for serving

SUGGESTED WINE:

PINOT GRIGIO RAMATO

Soak the noodles in cold tap water for 1 hour. Drain, cover the noodles to prevent drying and set aside. Meanwhile, roast the peanuts by baking a handful of peanuts on a sheet pan in a 325º oven until fragrant and lightly browned (or use store-bought roasted peanuts). When cool, place in a plastic bag and crush with a rolling pin or small skillet, then set aside. Make the sauce by combining the palm sugar, white sugar, tamarind water and fish sauce in a small saucepan. Simmer over low heat until the sugar is dissolved, then set aside. Heat a wok or large sauté pan over medium heat, add 2 tablespoons of the oil and fry the shallots until fragrant and golden, about 10 seconds. Add the shrimp and sauté for about 1 minute. Remove the shrimp to a plate and set aside to prevent overcooking. Crack the eggs into the pan and lightly break the yolks. Let the eggs fry for 2 minutes without stirring and then break into large pieces. Mix in the fried tofu, Roasted Thai Chili Flakes, dried shrimp and salted radish. Stir-fry until the tofu is heated through, about 1 minute, then add the soaked noodles. Adjust the heat to high, add the last tablespoon of oil and stir-fry the mixture for 3 to 5 minutes —folding the noodles over constantly until they become soft, translucent and light brown in color. Add the sauce and fold everything together for a few minutes until the sauce is mostly absorbed. Add the shrimp back to the pan. Add about ¾ of the bean sprouts and Chinese chives (reserving the rest for toppings) and cook for another 30 seconds. Transfer the Pad Thai to a serving platter and top with the crushed peanuts and the reserved chives and sprouts. Serve with lime wedges.

Pad See Ew

Stir-Fried Soy Sauce Noodles with Sirloin and Chinese Broccoli

SERVES 2

Pad See Ew is of Chinese origin. In fact, the migration of the Chinese into Thailand brought many dishes that we Thais now call our own. This is probably one of the most common street-food dishes you'll see in Thailand. It's almost always sold alongside its sister dish, Raat Naa (p. 122)—they're easy to share and they complement each other. Chinese broccoli is traditional here, but regular broccoli, bok choy, collard greens, zucchini or even cauliflower would be delicious.

- 8 oz. dried wide rice noodles
- 4 oz. sirloin, sliced into bite-size pieces
- 2 t. plus 3 T. light soy sauce, divided
- 2–3 T. plus 2 t. vegetable oil, divided
- 2 garlic cloves, minced
- 4 T. dark soy sauce
- 2 eggs
- 4 c. Chinese broccoli (or other vegetables), chopped
- 1–2 T. sugar
- Pinch ground white pepper
- Pickled Chilies (p. 161)

Soak the noodles in hot tap water for 1 hour. While the noodles are soaking, marinate the sirloin pieces in 2 teaspoons of the light soy sauce. When the noodles are soaked, drain and set aside, covered, to prevent them from drying. Heat a deep, wide pan over medium heat until hot and add 2 to 3 tablespoons of the oil. Once it shimmers, turn down the heat, add the garlic and sauté for 10 to 15 seconds, until fragrant and golden. Add the sirloin pieces and sauté until the meat is browned on the outside, about 2 minutes. Toss in the soaked noodles along with the rest of the light soy sauce and the dark soy sauce. Fold everything together, spread it out over the heated surface of the pan and wait about 20 seconds. Begin to stir-fry the noodles by folding them over several times for about 1 to 2 minutes—stirring the entire time—until the noodles are softened and have absorbed all the sauce. (If the noodles are taking a while to cook, add some chicken stock or water.) Make a well by moving the noodles to the sides of the pan. Add 2 teaspoons of oil, crack the eggs into the well, break the yolks and fry for 1 minute. When the eggs are partially cooked, flip them to cook the other side. Cook for 30 seconds, then mix the eggs with the noodles. Add the Chinese broccoli, stir and fold until wilted, about 1 to 2 minutes. Sprinkle with the sugar and mix well. Serve topped with white pepper and Pickled Chilies.

Raat Naa

Stir-Fried Noodles with Chicken, Chinese Broccoli and Gravy

SERVES 2

On the streets of Thailand, Raat Naa is almost always sold side-by-side with Pad See Ew (p. 120). The sister dishes have similar ingredients and the flavors are complementary, but unlike Pad See Ew, Raat Naa has a comforting gravy that's ladled over the warm, cooked noodles. My mom and I always order one Pad See Ew and one Raat Naa to share.

- 8 oz. dried flat rice noodles
- 3 oz. sliced chicken
- 2 t. plus 1 T. light soy sauce, divided
- 3 T. dark soy sauce, divided
- 4 T. vegetable oil, divided
- 2 t. minced garlic
- 1 c. Chicken Stock (p. 150)
- 2 t. sugar
- 1 T. salted soybean or soybean paste
- 1 T. tapioca flour
- 3 T. water
- 1 c. chopped Chinese broccoli (or substitute broccolini)
- Pickled Chilies (p. 161), for serving
- Roasted Thai Chili Flakes (p. 161), for serving

Soak the noodles in hot tap water for one hour, then drain and set aside. Marinate the chicken pieces with 2 teaspoons of the light soy sauce. Rub the drained noodles with 2 tablespoons of the dark soy sauce and let sit for 3 to 5 minutes. Heat a wok or deep sauté pan over medium heat and add 2 tablespoons of the oil. When the oil is hot, stir-fry the noodles until softened, about 1 to 2 minutes. (If the noodles are too firm to cook, add ¼ cup of water to help them steam.) Set aside. Add the remaining 2 tablespoons of oil to the wok and fry the garlic until golden, about 10 seconds. Add the chicken and stir-fry until it's halfway cooked, about 1 to 2 minutes. Add the stock and bring the mixture to a boil. Season with the remaining dark and light soy sauces, sugar and soybean paste and simmer for 3 minutes. In the meantime, make a slurry by mixing the tapioca flour with the water in a bowl. Add the slurry to the simmering stock and stir. Add the Chinese broccoli and simmer another minute or so until the broccoli is crisp-tender. Ladle the gravy and broccoli over the noodles and serve with sides of Pickled Chilies and Roasted Thai Chili Flakes.

Papaya Salad

SERVES 2

There's no talking about Thai street food without mentioning Papaya Salad—probably the king of street foods—and the sight of multiple vendors pounding away at salads in clay mortars is very familiar among Thais. There are several variations of Papaya Salad, but my favorite is the addition of fermented crab. If you're up for trying fermented crab, you can find it at most Asian markets. Another delicious variation is the salad topped with grilled prawns. It makes a nice presentation, and the combination of the sweet salad with the charred prawns is exquisite. Feel free to substitute cashews to make this salad peanut-free. The dressing is also very delicious served over mixed fruits.

FOR THE DRESSING:

2 T. palm sugar

1 T. tamarind water (p. 35)

1 T. water

2 T. fish sauce

1 T. lime juice

FOR THE SALAD:

1 T. dried shrimp

2 garlic cloves

Pinch salt

4–6 fresh Thai chilies (less or more according to your spice preference)

1 T. coarsely chopped roasted peanuts or cashews

4 cherry tomatoes, halved

2 snake beans, also known as Chinese long beans (or a small handful of snipped green beans)

2–3 c. shredded green papaya

1 c. fermented crab or 4–5 large grilled prawns (optional)

To make the dressing, heat the sugar, tamarind water and water in a small pan until the sugar is dissolved. Let the mixture cool, then add the fish sauce and lime juice, whisk and set aside.

Using a large clay mortar and wooden pestle, pound the dried shrimp until broken. Add the garlic, salt and chilies and pound until the garlic and chilies are broken into small pieces. Add the peanuts or cashews, tomatoes, snake or green beans and pound a few more times to bruise. Place the mixture in a bowl and add the shredded papaya. Add the dressing, toss and let sit for 5 to 10 minutes before serving. Serve the salad topped with the fermented crab or grilled prawns and with a side of sticky rice (p. 37) or coconut rice (p. 38).

PRO TIP

Don't Bruise the Papaya

Traditionally, the shredded papaya is added to the mortar and pounded. I've learned that making the salad this way overly bruises the papaya and it doesn't keep as long. If you're making this salad for a party, tossing the papaya with the dressing will help the salad keep longer—even for days in the fridge. Pounding the papaya is great if you're eating the salad immediately.

CHAPTER FIVE

In the Middle

Introducing Mom and Dad

My parents grew up in different parts of Thailand—my dad in southern Thailand, near the Malaysia border, and my mom in central Thailand, near Bangkok. Both learned to cook from their mothers, and both were influenced by their respective regional cuisines.

Southern Thailand has abundant seafood and lush coconut groves that inspire rich, creamy curries. Dishes tend to be spicier, and frequently include spices from both India and Malaysia. Central Thai cuisine focuses on a wealth of fresh vegetables and fruits, and the spices, sauces and preparations have a strong Chinese influence due to the great wave of Chinese immigrants that flocked to the region in the early 1900s.

Having grandparents and parents from different parts of the country diversified and shaped my palate from an early age. These are the dishes I grew up eating, and they always remind me of those times in the kitchen with both of my late grandmothers.

Dad's Simply Amazing Fried Chicken Wings with Sea Salt

SERVES 8

This recipe is a new one. It's the latest I learned from my dad during one of his recent visits to Austin. As soon as he arrived, he insisted he was going to make these chicken wings for me and he swore they would be a crowd-pleaser. *"Your cousin ate four pounds all by himself!"* he said. On Super Bowl Sunday, I brought him some chicken wings to cook, then busied myself getting other food ready for the party. When I returned, the cooked wings were almost gone! The crowd really went wild. The sizzling-hot wings seemed to pull in the salt—all the way to the bone—with no other seasoning or marinade necessary. Of course, you can get creative and add other dried spices to the salt, but given the simplicity of this recipe (and my dad's enthusiasm), I was so impressed I had to include it in this book. Thanks, Dad.

8 c. vegetable oil, or any oil with a high smoke-point

4 lb. chicken wing pieces (flats and drumettes)

1 T. fine sea salt, divided

SUGGESTED WINE:
SPARKLING RIESLING

Fill a large pot with about 6 inches of oil and heat to 350º. When the oil is hot, add the chicken in batches, starting with the drumettes—about 8 to 10 pieces at a time. Fry the pieces until they start to float to the surface and turn golden. As each batch finishes, remove to a large bowl lined with paper towels to absorb the excess oil, then toss with 1 teaspoon of the fine sea salt immediately while still very hot. Continue tossing each batch with salt as they finish frying.

Dad hard at work.

Kai Kolae

Southern-Style Grilled Chicken

SERVES 4–6

If you've visited markets in Southern Thailand, you've probably experienced this delicious charcoal-grilled marinated chicken, as well as the line of people eagerly waiting to get their hands on some. It has the flavors of a rich chicken curry, but the only sauce is the coating on the tender chicken. You won't miss the extra sauce, though, because this chicken is packed with flavor and perfect as is. It's one of the most aromatic grilled meats you'll ever smell or eat.

FOR THE MARINADE:

1 T. minced garlic

1 T. minced shallot

1 t. salt

1 T. minced ginger

1 T. minced cilantro stems or roots

1 t. ground white pepper

¼ c. coconut cream

1 whole chicken (about 2 lb.), split in half or spatchcocked whole (to spatchcock, remove the backbone with kitchen shears and flatten the chicken with the skin-side up)

FOR THE RED CURRY GRILLING SAUCE:

2 T. crushed roasted peanuts

2 c. coconut cream

½ c. Red Curry Paste (p. 41)

1 t. salt

¼ c. unsweetened coconut flakes

2 T. fish sauce

2 T. palm sugar

1 T. tamarind water (p. 35)

¼ c. thinly sliced ginger, for serving

Sprigs of cilantro, for serving

Hard-boiled eggs, for serving

Crisp Cucumber Relish (p. 155), for serving

SUGGESTED WINE:

DRY RIESLING

In a large bowl, mix together all of the marinade ingredients except for the chicken. Add the chicken to the bowl and coat with the marinade. Cover the bowl and refrigerate overnight.

Roast a handful of peanuts on a sheet pan in a 325º oven until fragrant and lightly browned (or use store-bought roasted peanuts). When the peanuts are cool, place in a bag and crush with a rolling pin or a small skillet. Set aside. Prepare a charcoal grill to medium-high heat. Meanwhile, bring the coconut cream to a boil on the stovetop and simmer until the cream and oil begin to separate, about 1 to 2 minutes. Add the curry paste and stir well to combine. Let the paste mixture simmer for about 3 minutes, until fragrant. Add the peanuts, salt and coconut flakes and simmer for an additional 2 minutes. Add the fish sauce, palm sugar and tamarind water and stir. Transfer the sauce to a casserole dish or sided platter (large enough to dip the chicken in) and set aside. Beginning with the skin side, grill the marinated chicken until brown and then flip to brown the other side, about 4 minutes per side. When both sides of the chicken are brown, carefully dip the chicken in the grilling sauce to coat on both sides and put it back on the grill for about 2 more minutes per side. Repeat the coating and grilling process 2 more times, until the chicken is cooked through. Serve with ginger, cilantro, hard-boiled eggs and Crisp Cucumber Relish.

Rice Soup with Pork

SERVES 4

A recent visit from my parents brought me renewed confidence in this recipe. I had made rice soup for my dad one night and he raved about it for the rest of his stay—he even begged me several times to make it again. He said it was the best rice soup he'd ever had. Little did he know, I'd used the exact recipe he'd taught me years ago. This soup is very simple, yet complex and hearty. I bet it becomes a family favorite.

1 T. vegetable oil
2 t. minced garlic
6 oz. ground pork
6 c. Chicken Stock (p. 150)
1½ c. cooked jasmine rice (p. 37)
3 T. light soy sauce, or more, to taste
¼ c. chopped cilantro leaves, for garnish
Ground white pepper, for garnish

Heat a saucepan over medium heat and add the oil. When the oil shimmers, add the fresh garlic and fry until golden, about 10 seconds. Add the pork and sauté until the meat is browning but not quite cooked through, about 1 minute. Add the stock, rice and soy sauce and let simmer for about 10 to 15 minutes, until the rice opens and becomes less grain-like. (Add more stock or water, if needed.) The soup should be thick, but with enough liquid to reach about 2 inches above the rice. Taste and adjust with more soy sauce, if needed. Garnish with the cilantro and white pepper and serve.

Coconut Vermicelli

SERVES 2

My mom came to visit when we first opened Thai Fresh in 2008. She was determined to write down this recipe for Coconut Vermicelli so I could make it at the restaurant. Six months went by, but she and I were both so busy, we never got around to it. Six months after that, she came back for a second visit, and making this dish was the first thing she wanted to do. I remember getting my pen and paper ready to write down what she did, but she kept quickly adding ingredients without measuring or telling me how much she put in. She apologized and explained that this was such a favorite dish from her childhood that making it was like being on autopilot. We had to start over, but that's okay. I eventually got the recipe down. If you'd like to make this dish with meat or seafood, use ½ cup of sliced raw chicken or shrimp when you would have added the tofu.

- 2 T. vegetable oil
- 1 T. minced shallot
- 2 t. minced cilantro stems
- ½ c. fried tofu (p. 44), cut into ½-inch x ¼-inch pieces
- 1 c. coconut milk
- 2 T. ketchup
- 2 T. tamarind water (p. 35)
- 1 T. palm sugar
- 1–2 T. fish or soy sauce
- 2 t. soybean paste
- 4 oz. dried vermicelli noodles (I like Wai Wai brand), soaked for 30 minutes in cold tap water, drained
- ¼ c. Chinese chives (sometimes called garlic chives), cut into 1½-inch pieces
- ½ c. bean sprouts

Heat a deep sauté pan over medium heat and add the oil. When the oil is hot, add the shallot and cilantro stems and stir-fry until fragrant—about 10 seconds. Add the fried tofu and cook for 1 minute. Add the coconut milk, ketchup, tamarind water, palm sugar, fish or soy sauce and soybean paste and mix well. Bring the mixture to a simmer and let it cook for 1 minute. Add the drained noodles and mix until the sauce is absorbed by the noodles. Fold in the chives and bean sprouts, remove from the heat and serve.

SUGGESTED WINE:
FRENCH PINOT BLANC

Kao Yum

Rainbow Rice Salad

SERVES 6

Kao Yum, literally "rice salad," is another true southern Thai favorite. The rice is often made using dried butterfly pea flowers (found online) giving it the most beautiful blue hue, but you can use plain rice if you like. The real star here, in my opinion, is the dressing. I grew up eating this traditional dish, but my version makes it easier for those without access to the fermented fish sauce that's used in Southern Thailand. I've swapped it for shrimp paste, which I think has a similar flavor profile.

FOR THE DRESSING:

3 c. water
1 T. minced garlic
1 shallot, chopped
2 T. thinly sliced lemongrass
2 T. chopped galangal
4 makrut lime leaves, torn
4 oz. salted mackerel in oil, broken into pieces
2 T. shrimp paste
2 T. palm sugar
½ t. lime juice

FOR THE RICE AND SALAD:

⅓ c. coconut flakes
4 c. uncooked jasmine rice
6 c. water
1 T. dried butterfly pea flowers
1 c. thinly sliced green beans
½ c. ground salted shrimp
½ c. shredded unripe mango (found at Asian markets, not the green mangoes found at regular grocery stores)
¼ c. julienned makrut lime leaves
⅓ c. julienned Thai basil
⅓ c. chopped dill
1 c. sunflower sprouts

To make the dressing, combine the water, garlic, shallot, lemongrass, galangal and lime leaves in a saucepan and bring to a boil. Reduce the heat and simmer for a few minutes, then add the salted fish pieces and continue to simmer for 15 more minutes. Strain the liquid through a fine-mesh strainer—reserving the liquid but discarding the solids. Season the dressing by whisking in the shrimp paste, palm sugar and lime juice. Set aside to cool.

To make the rice and salad, first toast the coconut flakes on a small baking sheet in a 325º oven until fragrant and slightly browned. Set aside. Combine the rice, water and butterfly pea flowers in a large pot. Stir well and bring to a boil. Reduce the heat to a low simmer, cover and cook for 15 minutes. Turn off the heat but keep the rice covered for another 10 minutes. After 10 minutes, remove the butterfly pea flowers. To serve, heap the rice onto individual plates, portion out the green beans, salted shrimp, mango, lime leaves, coconut flakes, basil, dill and sprouts to each plate and mix in about 2 to 3 tablespoons of the dressing per plate.

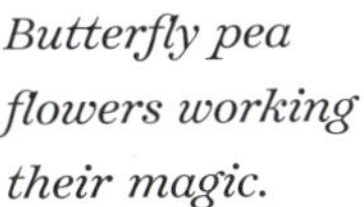

Butterfly pea flowers working their magic.

Panang Curry with Beef

SERVES 4–6

My students have often asked why I don't add any vegetables to my Panang Curry. My other curries feature vegetables, so why not this one? My simple answer has always been that I'd never eaten Panang Curry with vegetables in my entire life. My mom made it only with beef, and that's the way I thought it should be made. But as a cooking instructor, I wanted to dig deeper for my students and really think about it. Why were there never any veggies added to Panang Curry? My conclusion is that the brightness of this curry comes from the amount and type of spices added. It's basically a red curry base, but with the addition of a few key flavors like peanuts and nutmeg. When vegetables are added to a dish, the background spices can become muted, diluted or even overpowered—sometimes you want that balancing act. But I think Panang Curry would end up tasting like a basic red curry with vegetables, which is not a bad thing, just not what we're looking for here. Save the veggies for a side dish and let this curry shine the way it was intended. Be sure to use a fattier cut of beef for the longer simmering time. If you don't have time to make my homemade Panang Curry Paste, I recommend a 4-ounce can of the Maesri brand panang curry paste as a good substitute.

FOR THE PANANG CURRY PASTE:

½ c. peanuts

½ t. cumin seeds

½ t. coriander seeds

1 piece nutmeg (about ⅛ of a whole nutmeg)

1 T. minced lemongrass

1½ T. minced galangal

10 large dried red Thai chilies, seeded, soaked for 20 minutes in warm water, chopped

¼ c. chopped shallots

10 garlic cloves, chopped

1 t. salt

1 t. makrut lime zest

1 t. minced cilantro roots (or 5 cilantro stems, minced)

1 t. shrimp paste

Roast the peanuts on a sheet pan in a 325º oven until fragrant and slightly golden (or use store-bought roasted peanuts). When cool, chop, measure out 4 tablespoons and set aside. Toast the cumin seeds, coriander seeds and nutmeg separately in a dry pan over medium heat. Move 1 ingredient around until fragrant, then remove and toast the next. Using a large mortar and pestle, pound 1 ingredient at a time—beginning with the roasted peanuts and toasted seeds—in the order listed. Pound each ingredient until it's mostly ground before adding the next. When you get to the chilies, shallots and garlic, add the salt and pound (the salt helps absorb moisture and prevent splattering). Finally, add the lime zest, cilantro and shrimp paste. (Alternatively, double the amount of the ingredients and use a powerful blender, like a Vitamix.) The paste can be stored in the refrigerator for up to 1 month, but do not freeze.

(continued on following page)

FOR THE CURRY:

2 13½-oz. unshaken cans coconut milk

1 recipe Panang Curry Paste

2½ lb. rump or chuck roast, cut into ¼-inch slices

2 T. fish sauce

2 T. sugar

6 makrut lime leaves, torn

1 c. whole Thai basil leaves

Cooked jasmine rice (p. 37), for serving

Scoop the cream from the top half of the unshaken cans of coconut milk into a large saucepan and bring to a boil over medium heat. Lower the heat to a simmer and cook for 1 minute. Add the curry paste and mix until completely smooth and combined. Turn the heat to low and simmer the mixture, without stirring, until fragrant and the coconut cream begins to release some oil, about 3 to 5 minutes. (Remember not to stir because that would lower the temperature and the paste would not fry correctly.) Add the beef slices to the mixture and simmer for 5 minutes, stirring occasionally. Add the rest of the coconut milk and bring back to boil. Reduce the heat to low and simmer the beef for 45 minutes. Season with the fish sauce and sugar. Taste and adjust the seasoning, if needed. Add the lime and basil leaves and turn off the heat. Serve with jasmine rice.

PRO TIP

Store-Bought Paste

If you don't have time to make my homemade Panang Curry Paste, I recommend two 4-ounce cans of the Maesri brand panang curry paste as a good substitute.

Orange Curry

with Grouper and Turnips

SERVES 4

Orange Curry is a staple in our family. Despite the name, there are no oranges involved; it's all about the final color. This is probably the very first curry that I felt confident enough to make without my mom's supervision. When I was a young girl in Thailand, I made it for my dad almost every single weekend before I left for my public-speaking club—it was a ritual. I like to add turmeric to the paste because that's the way my grandma in the south of Thailand made it. My mom has also adopted the addition of turmeric. You don't need coconut milk for this curry and it's very versatile—add any vegetables you like!

5 dried long red Thai chilies, seeded and soaked for 20 minutes in warm water, then chopped

5 dried small red Thai chilies

½ t. salt

½ c. chopped shallots

2 garlic cloves

1 t. shrimp paste

2 t. chopped fresh turmeric root (optional)

3 T. fish sauce, divided

6 oz. grouper (or any flaky, light fish like cod or flounder)

3 c. water

2 c. bite-size turnip cubes, (or a mix of turnip, carrot and cauliflower)

2 T. tamarind water (p. 35)

1 t. palm sugar

Cooked jasmine rice (p. 37), for serving

Using a mortar and pestle, make a paste by pounding together the first 7 ingredients (through the turmeric root), 1 at a time, in the order listed. (Alternatively, you could use a food processor for this paste). Add 1 tablespoon of the fish sauce to the paste, then softly bruise and break up half of the fish into the paste using the pestle. Don't mash the fish, just gently press and separate. (If using a food processor, pulse the fish with the paste a few times.) Meanwhile, bring the water to a boil in a large pot. Add the paste and the rest of the fish to the water and simmer for about 2 minutes. Remove the fish but keep the water simmering. Add the turnip cubes and simmer for about 10 minutes. Add the tamarind water, the rest of the fish sauce and the palm sugar. Put the fish back in the pot, adjust the seasoning if needed, remove from the heat and serve over jasmine rice.

Mom's Fried Beef Jerky

with Spicy Lime Sauce

SERVES 6

One very vivid memory from childhood is my mom carefully placing pieces of marinated beef onto bamboo trays to be dried in the backyard sun. We knew that great snacks were just two sun cycles away, because in the hot, humid climate of Thailand, we could depend on direct sun, with occasional, almost predictable, clouds drifting in at certain times of the day. The beef pieces were flipped after the first clouds covered the sun, and the meat was done when the second clouds came through—about an hour of sun on each side. Most of the time, Mom fried the pieces before freezing them; the simple flavor of the marinated beef turns rich and complex after being fried. The sauce makes the perfect dip.

FOR THE SAUCE:

3 T. lime juice

2 T. fish sauce

1 t. sugar

¼ t. (or more) Roasted Thai Chili Flakes (p. 161)

1 shallot, sliced thinly

1 T. chopped cilantro

FOR THE JERKY:

3 T. light soy sauce

1 T. whiskey (optional)

2 t. sugar

1 lb. beef roast, cut into 3-inch x ¼-inch strips, about ⅛-inch thick

3 c. vegetable oil, for deep-frying

Sticky rice, for serving (p. 39)

Spicy Lime Sauce, for serving

To make the sauce, whisk together all of the ingredients and set aside.

In a large bowl, mix together the soy sauce, whiskey (if using) and sugar. Add the beef pieces and marinate for about 30 minutes. To dry the beef, you can use my mom's method of putting the pieces on a rack or basket and drying in the sun—about 2 hours total, flipping halfway through. Or, heat the oven to 200º and bake for 15 minutes. Alternatively, you can dry the beef in a dehydrator if you have one. The surface of the beef pieces should be dry but not so dry that they stick to the rack. To fry, heat the oil to 350º in a deep-frying pan. Fry the beef until it's cooked through—about 1 to 2 minutes. Serve with sticky rice and Spicy Lime Sauce.

Ginger Stir-Fry

with Pork and Wood Ear Mushroom

SERVES 2–4

My mom always told us that as we got older, we would start to like different flavors—even surprisingly bold ones that may not have seemed that palatable at first. That is certainly the case with this dish. It has a LOT of ginger. As a kid, I would try it every time my mom made it, and the more I tried it, the more I grew to love it. I acquired a taste for it, and now it makes me feel like I'm home every time I make it. My dad loves this with ground pork, and I do, too. But you can use other meats if you prefer. Even though this dish is ginger-heavy, every flavor complements each other; the fermented soybean paste (found at Asian markets) is particularly amazing. This is salty and sweet with a pronounced ginger bite.

- 1 c. fresh ginger matchsticks (see method on right)
- 2 T. vegetable oil
- 2 garlic cloves, minced
- ½ c. ground pork
- ½ c. sliced yellow onions
- ½ c. chopped wood ear mushrooms (also called fungus mushrooms), either fresh or dried (if dried, soak in warm water for 20 minutes before using)
- ¼–½ c. Chicken Stock (p. 150)
- 1 T. fish sauce
- 1 T. dark soy sauce
- 2 t. fermented soybean paste
- 1 T. sugar
- 2 green onions (green and white parts), chopped into 1½-inch pieces

Slice a 3-inch long piece of ginger (no need to peel) lengthwise into ⅛-inch thick planks. Stack the planks and slice them into very thin matchsticks. Heat a deep sauté pan over high heat. Lower the heat to medium, add the oil and fry the garlic until fragrant—about 10 seconds. Add the pork—breaking up the meat into pieces—and sauté until it's mostly cooked—about 2 minutes. Add the onions, mushrooms and ginger matchsticks and sauté for 2 minutes. Add the stock to moisten as you stir. Add the fish sauce, soy sauce, fermented soybean paste and sugar, and mix well. Turn off the heat and fold in the green onions until slightly wilted—about 10 seconds. Serve with rice.

PRO TIP

Just a Splash or So

When stir-frying anything other than rice or noodles, add a splash of water or stock as the mixture becomes dry. Liquid will help moisten the food and create steam to speed up the cooking process. Add more as needed, just a splash at a time, but avoid boiling the food. Stir-fries should have some sauce left on the bottom of the pan. You know the seasoning is right when you taste the sauce. Adjust as needed.

Whole Fish with Turmeric, Garlic and Ginger

SERVES 4

Bright-golden turmeric root is an amazing ingredient. It's beneficial for our health, and it also happens to taste great. In Thai cuisine, we use fresh turmeric root almost exclusively—you hardly ever see the powdered form. The root is minced or grated, then pounded into a paste and mixed with other spices ("turmeric hand" is a common and welcomed affliction in my family). I have tried many different types of fish with this recipe and had great success. My favorite fish to use is lane snapper or striped bass. You can also use bone-in pieces of fish instead of whole for easier frying.

- 3 T. minced fresh turmeric root, divided
- 1 T. salt
- 3 T. minced garlic, divided
- 2 T. minced ginger, divided
- 1–2 whole, bone-in lane snappers or 1 striped bass (about 2 lb. of fish, total), cleaned, gutted
- 4¼ c. vegetable oil, divided
- ¼ c. chopped cilantro stems, for garnish
- The ULTIMATE Sauce (p. 159), for serving

SUGGESTED WINE:
CHENIN BLANC

Using a large mortar and pestle, pound together 2 tablespoons of the turmeric, all of the salt, 2 tablespoons of the garlic and 1 tablespoon of the ginger to make a paste. Score the fish with two slits on each side and rub the paste all over the fish, inside and out. Let the fish sit in the fridge for 2 hours. In a large, deep pan, heat 4 cups of the oil to 350º. Deep-fry the fish for 8 to 10 minutes, until golden. (Peek through the slits to see if the fish is cooked through.) Remove the fish to a paper towel-lined platter. Heat the remaining ¼ cup of oil in a small saucepan and add the remaining tablespoons of turmeric, garlic and ginger. Fry the ingredients until fragrant and golden, then drizzle the fried spices and oil over the fish. Garnish with the cilantro and serve with The ULTIMATE Sauce on the side for dipping.

Steamed Mussels with Red Curry and Pineapple

SERVES 4

This version of red curry was not common in Thailand when I was growing up, unless you were in my family's kitchen. Pineapple adds the perfect pop of tang and sweet to balance out the brine of the mussels and the fire of the curry. Earthy black pepper replaces the Thai basil usually found in red curry. Feel free to substitute clams or scallops, if you like.

2 c. water

4 lb. fresh mussels

1 13½-oz. unshaken can of coconut milk

¼ c. Red Curry Paste (p. 41)

2 c. small-dice fresh pineapple

2 T. fish sauce

1 t. sugar

½ t. freshly ground black pepper

4 makrut lime leaves, torn into ½-inch pieces

Cooked jasmine rice, for serving (p. 37)

Heat the water in a large, lidded stockpot over medium heat. When the water is simmering, add the mussels, place the lid on the pot and cook until the shells open—about 3 to 5 minutes. Discard any mussels that didn't open. Remove the mussels from the shells and set aside (you should end up with about 1½ cups of mussels).

Scoop out the creamy top half of the unshaken can of coconut milk, place in a medium saucepan and bring to a boil. Let the cream simmer for about 1 minute, until the surface starts to shine. Add the curry paste and stir. Turn the heat to medium-high and let the mixture simmer for about 3 to 4 minutes, until fragrant. (You'll start to see some red oil floating to the surface of the curry.) Add the rest of coconut milk and bring to a boil. Lower the heat to simmer, add the pineapple pieces and simmer for about 10 minutes, until the pineapple is caramelized. (The color of the curry will get a little darker when the pineapple is finished caramelizing.) Add the mussels and let them simmer for 1 or 2 minutes. Add the fish sauce, sugar, black pepper and lime leaves and stir to combine. Turn off the heat and serve with jasmine rice.

CHAPTER SIX

Foundational Elements

Sauces, Condiments and the Good Funk

There are some key ingredients in Thai cuisine that are used to complement or enhance other flavors in a dish—often providing a needed texture or introducing a missing element in the all-important "five-flavor combo." Some of these "enhancers" are delicious on their own, like my Crisp Cucumber Relish or Pickled Cabbage. Some are meant to be drizzled over foods, like my Homemade Sriracha Sauce. And some appear as condiments for a last-minute finish at the table. (My dad is known to carry his own stash of my ULTIMATE Sauce with him to restaurants.) These ingredients have a foundational value based on what they bring—whether it's a bright pop of sour, an umami saltiness or what I like to call "the good funk." Most importantly, they're versatile and can be applied and enjoyed across multiple cuisines.

Chicken Stock

MAKES ABOUT 12 CUPS

Discovering the method for making this chicken stock was probably one of the most eye-opening experiences I've had so far as a cook. My dad had bought me this little Thai book on chef secrets when I first opened Thai Fresh, but I was so busy with the restaurant, I didn't pick it up until six months or so later. When I finally opened it, I flipped to the page on making chicken stock and laughed. I thought there was just no way this method could work. At the time, my "recipe" was to boil a whole chicken forever until it fell apart. The stock ended up absolutely fine, but the chicken ended up a little bit over-cooked. Just for the heck of it, I tried this new "secret" method with no hope or faith that it would work, but I was amazed at how it turned out. The chicken was tender to the bone and the breast meat moist and usable. But the best part was that the stock took a mere 25 minutes to cook instead of hours! Of course, using the freshest local chicken you can find will also add distinct richness and depth to the final flavor.

1 whole chicken (about 3 lb.)
3 garlic cloves, crushed
5 ginger slices (¼-inch thick each)
10 cilantro stems
2 t. salt

Place all of the ingredients in a large stockpot and add just enough water to cover. Bring to a boil, then reduce the heat to low, cover and let simmer for 25 minutes. Remove the chicken to a platter to cool. Strain the stock through a fine-mesh strainer, discard the solids and either use the stock immediately or set it aside to cool. When the chicken is cool enough to handle, remove and discard the skin, then pull and/or slice the meat from the bones and use in other recipes. Once the stock is cool, refrigerate it for use in the next few days or freeze it for up to 3 months.

PRO TIP

Skip the Skim

Unlike many recipes for making stock, this one doesn't call for skimming the surface of the pot as it simmers.

Salted Duck Eggs

MAKES 5 EGGS

You can find salted duck eggs at most Asian markets, but my dad likes to make them at home because they're so easy. After the eggs have been salted (note: this takes 2 to 3 weeks), you hard-boil them just as you would a chicken egg. Salted eggs are delicious crumbled into Crab Fried Rice (p. 67), or quartered and mixed with thinly sliced shallots and cilantro and topped with The ULTIMATE Sauce (p. 159) for a dressed duck-egg salad. Remember that these eggs are salty, so reduce the amount of salt in your recipe.

8 c. water

2 T. salt

5 fresh duck eggs

Bring the water and salt to a boil, then let cool completely. Place the duck eggs in a large mason jar and pour the saltwater over the eggs, filling to the top of the jar. Break a bamboo skewer or chopstick to fit snugly inside the jar opening and place it above the eggs to prevent them from floating above the water. Screw on the lid and label the jar with the date. Let the jar sit at room temperature for 21 days, then remove the eggs and store in the fridge. (For less salty eggs, remove the eggs from the water after 14 days.) When you're ready to eat the eggs, hard-boil them exactly as you would chicken eggs, cut in half, scoop out of the shell and enjoy.

Keeping the eggs submerged.

Thai Chili Jam

MAKES 4 CUPS

This spicy-sweet chili jam is a staple in many Thai kitchens and is so versatile. Use it to finish soups, to stir-fry veggies or seafood or as a tangy dipping sauce for fresh or steamed veggies. It also provides the perfect flavor profile to complement fried rice. It's only mildly spicy, but you can adjust the heat by adding more chilies, if you like.

1 t. shrimp paste

½ c. concentrated tamarind water

2 c. vegetable oil

2 c. thinly sliced shallots

1 c. thinly sliced garlic

¼ c. dried shrimp

½ c. dried long red Thai chilies, seeded, chopped (or substitute dried New Mexico chilies, such as Hatch or Anaheim)

5 slices galangal, about ⅛-inch thick

½ c. palm sugar

2 t. salt or 3 T. fish sauce

Place the shrimp paste on a large spoon and hold it over an open flame on the stovetop for 1 to 2 minutes. (The spoon gets hot, so use a potholder.) If you don't have an open-flame stove, fold the shrimp paste in a small aluminum foil packet and heat in a hot dry pan on the stovetop—turning a few minutes to evenly roast. Set aside.

Next, make the concentrated tamarind water by soaking ⅓-cup scoop of seedless tamarind pulp (available at Asian markets) in ¾ cup slightly warm water for 15 minutes. Squeeze out, strain and reserve the liquid. Add more water to the leftover solids, if needed, and press and strain to make ½ cup. Set aside.

To make the jam, heat the oil in a medium-size saucepan over medium heat. One at a time, deep-fry the shallots, then the garlic, then the dried shrimp, chilies and galangal until golden—removing to drain on paper towels as you go. Blend all the fried ingredients with the roasted shrimp paste in a food processor—adding a bit of the frying oil, up to ½ cup, to moisten the mixture. Heat the blended mixture in a saucepan over medium heat and season with the palm sugar, tamarind water and salt or fish sauce. Simmer until quite thick—stirring regularly to prevent burning. The finished jam should be sweet, sour and salty with a little kick. The jam will keep in the refrigerator for 3 months, and freezes well.

Nam Prik Kapi

Shrimp Paste Relish

SERVES 6

This relish isn't as common in the U.S. as other Thai relishes, but it's so close to my heart that I had to include it here. It's deeply connected to memories from my childhood: my family sitting around our table enjoying the relish with fresh veggies from our garden. You can make this so spicy your pores will open up while you're eating it, or you can make it less spicy and enjoy it without many tears. It goes well with fresh or steamed vegetables and makes a great presentation at parties. It's a tasty way to introduce a very old, truly traditional Thai relish to friends.

1 T. shrimp paste, roasted
5 garlic cloves
⅛ t. salt
3–5 fresh Thai chilies, red or green
2 t. palm sugar
1 T. lime juice
1 t. fish sauce

To roast the shrimp paste, place it on a large spoon and hold it over a flame on the stovetop for 1 to 2 minutes. (The spoon will get hot, so use a potholder.) If you don't have an open-flame stove, fold the shrimp paste in a small aluminum foil packet and heat in a hot dry pan on the stovetop—turning after a few minutes to evenly roast. Next, pound together the garlic, salt and roasted shrimp paste using a mortar and pestle (or small food processor, being careful not to overprocess). Add the chilies one at a time and pound until they are bruised and broken into smaller pieces (we want chunky). Add the palm sugar, lime juice and fish sauce and mix well. Spoon the relish over your favorite vegetables and serve.

Crisp Cucumber Relish

MAKES 3 CUPS

This quick and refreshing relish is served with many Thai dishes, including Chicken Satay (p. 71) and Massaman Curry (p. 180). It doesn't keep very long before getting soggy, so make it the day you need it and use any leftovers within 3 days. This is another great way to add the "five-flavor combo" (p. 27) to a dish.

- 1/3 c. white vinegar
- 1/3 c. sugar
- 1/2 c. water
- 1 t. salt
- 3 pickling cucumbers (small, fat cucumbers), quartered, sliced into 1/8-inch thick pieces
- 1 serrano pepper, thinly sliced
- 1 shallot, thinly sliced
- 1 t. peeled, minced ginger
- 1/4 c. chopped cilantro

In a medium saucepan, bring the vinegar, sugar, water and salt to a boil. Dissolve the sugar, then turn off the heat and let cool. Once the liquid is cool, combine all of the ingredients in a bowl and toss well. Let the relish rest for 20 minutes before serving. It can be served at room temperature or chilled.

Toasted Ground Sticky Rice

MAKES ABOUT 1 CUP

Larb (p. 116) is the main dish Thais make that includes Toasted Ground Sticky Rice—without it, it just wouldn't taste authentic.

- 1 c. uncooked Thai sticky rice (also called "sweet rice" or "glutinous rice," although still gluten-free)
- 2 slices galangal, bruised with the back of a knife
- 1/4 c. lemongrass pieces (1/2-inch pieces from about 1/2 stalk) tough outer layer removed, bruised with the back of a knife

Heat a medium pan over medium-high heat. When the pan is hot, lower the heat to medium and add the rice, galangal and lemongrass pieces. Move the ingredients around until the rice is evenly browned, about 10 minutes. Turn off the heat and let cool. Grind in batches in a spice grinder or food processor, then store in an airtight container in the pantry for up to 6 months, or in the freezer for up to a year.

Fried Thai Chilies
Crisp Cucumber Relish
Thai Chili Jam
Nam Prik Kapi

Sweet-and-Sour
Sauce
Homemade
Sriracha
Sauce
The ULTIMATE
Sauce
Salted Duck Eggs

Sweet-and-Sour Sauce

MAKES 1½ CUPS

This is the classic sauce served with fried egg rolls, but it goes great with other fried foods, as well. I also serve it with stir-fried noodle dishes and with my Spicy Red Curry Rice Balls (p. 194).

½ c. water
1 c. sugar
½ c. white vinegar
1 t. salt
1 T. minced garlic
1 t. Roasted Thai Chili Flakes (p. 161)

In a small, heavy saucepan, combine the water, sugar, vinegar and salt and bring to a rolling boil over medium heat. Stir to dissolve the sugar and salt, and reduce the heat to low. Simmer until the liquid thickens slightly to a light syrup—about 5 minutes. Add the garlic and Roasted Thai Chili Flakes, turn off the heat and cool to room temperature. Store in the refrigerator for up to 3 months.

The Perfect Marinade

MAKES ABOUT 1½ CUPS

At Thai Fresh, we use this basic marinade for the majority of our grilled, deep-fried and roasted meats (I usually marinate whole chickens overnight. For pieces of bone-in chicken or pork, I marinate for 4 hours; boneless meat gets 2 hours.) Different cooking methods will bring out different flavor profiles from the marinade. Using a mortar and pestle to make the marinade is best, but if you don't have one, mince the ingredients and use a blender.

6 garlic cloves, minced
1 T. freshly ground white or black pepper
3 T. minced cilantro leaves
½ t. salt
1 c. light soy sauce
1 T. sugar

Use a large mortar and pestle to pound together the garlic, pepper, cilantro and salt. Once incorporated, add the soy sauce and sugar and stir.

The ULTIMATE Sauce

MAKES ½ CUP

If you don't make anything else in this book, make this sauce! It's not complicated, and the flavor profile completely represents the beauty and simplicity of Thai cuisine. Years ago, I was invited to an oyster party, and I brought 2 quarts of this sauce for topping the fresh oysters. The sauce disappeared in what seemed like seconds—everyone was raving! Now, it's my go-to dipping/topping sauce for raw, grilled, fried or steamed seafood. But I've also used it to top grilled steak, and after slightly diluting with water, as a salad dressing. Make it!

1 T. minced garlic

2 t. minced fresh Thai chilies, red or green

1 T. minced cilantro stems

¼ t. salt

1 t. sugar or honey

4 T. lime juice

3 T. fish sauce

Whisk everything together in a bowl and serve with everything from oysters to a shoe.

Homemade Sriracha Sauce

MAKES ABOUT 1½ CUPS

Sriracha is the name of a town on the eastern seaboard of Thailand, where this sauce is said to have originated. As the story goes, the sauce was originally of Vietnamese origin, but was adapted using spicier Thai peppers. The fresh peppers used in this recipe are hard to find in the U.S., but many long red or orange chilies will work. Experiment with different peppers and see what you like.

10 long red Thai chilies, fresh or dried (fresh red serrano peppers are a good substitution, or use dried arbol chilies), seeded, chopped

1 c. whole garlic cloves

1 t. salt

¼ c. sugar

1½ c. water

3 T. white vinegar

Combine the chilies, garlic, salt, sugar and water in a saucepan. Bring to a boil and simmer until the chilies and garlic are tender—about 5 to 7 minutes. Let the mixture cool, then add the vinegar and puree in a blender until smooth. Store in the refrigerator for up to 3 months.

Thai Chilies in
Fish Sauce
Roasted Thai
Chili Flakes
Pickled Chilies

On the Thai Table

These three condiments are staples on restaurant tables in Thailand, as well as here and around the world. They each bring their own magic—adding that little something salty, sour or spicy needed for an umami boost. They're easy to make, and they keep well.

Thai Chilies in Fish Sauce

MAKES 1 CUP

1 c. sliced small fresh Thai chilies, green and red (about ⅛-inch pieces)

Fish sauce, to cover

Place the chilies in a lidded glass jar, cover with the fish sauce and let sit for at least 2 hours. The spiciness of the chilies will soften the longer they sit in the sauce. Refrigerate for up to 3 months.

Pickled Chilies

MAKES 1 CUP

1 c. sliced green or red serrano peppers (about ¼-inch pieces)

White vinegar, to cover

Place the chilies in a lidded glass jar, cover with the vinegar and set aside to pickle at room temperature for 1 day. After 1 day, refrigerate for up to 6 months.

Roasted Thai Chili Flakes

MAKES ABOUT 1 CUP

Use these flakes whenever you want something to be "no fooling around" spicy. Unlike common crushed red-pepper flakes found in the U.S., these pack a serious wallop, so use with caution. Alternatively, you could use dried arbol chilies found at most grocery stores. The flakes will be less spicy, but not by much. Roasting the chilies brings out more depth and flavor, but it also releases capsaicin molecules, which can irritate your lungs and mucous membranes, so roast in a well-ventilated area.

1 8-oz. bag small dried Thai chilies

Heat the oven to 350º and open the windows. Place the chilies on a sheet pan and roast them until fragrant (or until you start to cough if you're by the oven)—about 3 to 5 minutes. (Alternatively, you could toast the chilies in a dry pan over medium heat on the stovetop, but hold your breath.) The chilies will look shiny and darker red as they roast. Once the chilies are cool enough to handle, grind them in a food processor and store in an airtight container in the pantry.

Candied Pork Belly

SERVES 4

1 lb. pork belly slab, skin on

¼ c. vegetable oil

1 c. thinly sliced shallots

½ c. palm sugar

2 T. dark soy sauce

¼ c. light soy sauce

½ c. water

Cut the pork belly into ¼-thick strips lengthwise and then into about 2-inch pieces (or into ¼-inch pieces if using for Kao Klook Kapi (p. 65)). Heat a deep sauté pan over medium heat until hot and add the oil. When the oil shimmers, add the shallots and fry until they're a little bit brown and fragrant. Add the palm sugar and let it simmer on low heat for about 2 minutes, until slightly thickened. Increase the heat to medium-low, add the pork belly pieces and sauté for 2 minutes. Season with the dark and light soy sauces and add the water. Let the mixture simmer at low heat for about 10 more minutes—adding more water, if needed. (It should be thick and a little saucy.) Turn off the heat and use in your favorite dishes or serve over rice.

Crispy Pork Belly

MAKES ABOUT 2 POUNDS

Even though pork belly is a relatively new culinary darling in the U.S., Thais have been eating and loving it for a very long time. We typically prepare it two ways at Thai Fresh: crispy and candied. Our Crispy Pork Belly is very popular as the protein for different stir-fries, or simply served over rice with a sour sauce (recipe below) and fresh cucumber slices. We serve Candied Pork Belly as a side item for certain rice dishes like Kao Klook Kapi (p. 65).

4 c. water

2 lb. pork belly slab, cut into about 6-inch wide pieces, skin on

¼ c. white vinegar

1 T. dark soy sauce

1 T. salt

FOR THE SOUR SAUCE:

2 T. dark soy sauce

½ c. white vinegar

1 t. salt

1 T. sugar

2 jalapeño or serrano peppers, thinly sliced

In a large, wide saucepan, bring the water and pork belly pieces to a boil. Simmer for 30 minutes, remove the pork belly—reserving the water—and set the pieces on a cooling rack over a large bowl. Add the vinegar to the water and bring back to a boil. Carefully ladle the vinegar water over the pork pieces, flip and repeat a few times using the water that's collected in the bowl. Remove the pork belly to a plate and prick all over with a fork. Rub the pieces with the dark soy sauce and salt, place them back on the rack and let them air-dry. (Using a fan can speed the process.) Turn the pieces over once to dry the other side. Heat the oven to 350º and roast the pork belly pieces, skin-side down, on a rack over a sheet tray to catch the oil, until golden—about 1 hour. Cut the pieces into cubes to use in stir-fries or to serve over rice with sour sauce and fresh cucumber slices.

To make the sauce, combine all of the ingredients but the peppers in a saucepan and bring to a boil to dissolve the sugar. Remove from the heat, add the peppers and let cool before serving.

Pickled Cabbage

MAKES 2 CUPS

I adapted this old Thai recipe for pickling cabbage to make it easier for home cooks, but the recipe remains true to classic Thai flavors. It's a quick and easy way to create a bright side dish that goes well with everything from sandwiches and soups to fried rice.

1 T. stemmed, seeded, chopped dried long red Thai chilies (or substitute dried guajillo chilies)

1 t. salt

1 T. chopped shallot

1 T. chopped garlic

¼ c. vegetable oil

1 c. coconut water (fresh or canned)

1 c. white vinegar

1 c. shredded or julienned carrots

3 c. shredded cabbage, white or green

1 T. white sugar

1 t. toasted sesame seeds

Make a smooth paste by pounding together the chilies, salt, shallot and garlic using a mortar and pestle. (Alternatively, mince all of the ingredients very fine). Heat the oil in a large frying pan over medium heat until the oil shimmers. Turn down the heat to medium-low, add the paste and fry until fragrant—about 20 seconds. Add the coconut water and vinegar and bring to a boil. Add the carrots and cabbage and cook for 1 minute, until wilted (be careful not to overcook). Add the sugar, mix well, taste and add more salt, if needed. Sprinkle with the sesame seeds and serve. This is best when eaten on the same day but will keep in the fridge for up to 7 days.

Pictured is a pulled-pork sandwich using the cooked pork from Kao Ka Moo (p. 107). Shred the pork, place it on a toasted bun and top with the pickled cabbage.

Pickled Chinese Cabbage

MAKES ABOUT 2 POUNDS

Pickled Chinese Cabbage appears on the side of many dishes in Thai and Chinese cuisine. It's very simple to make, and adds that balance of sour and salty flavors to dishes that lean toward the sweet and spicy. Use this recipe to experiment with other Chinese greens found at your local farmers market.

FOR THE SOAK:

2 lb. Chinese cabbage (also known as Napa cabbage)

¾ c. salt

5 c. water

FOR THE PICKLING:

4 c. water

¼ c. brown sugar

2 T. uncooked jasmine rice

2 T. sea salt

Wash, stack and quarter the cabbage leaves (if it's a very large head, cut the leaves smaller), and place them in a large glass or plastic container. In a medium mixing bowl or large measuring cup, mix the salt with the water and stir until the salt is dissolved. Add the saltwater to the cabbage, and use something heavy, like a plate stacked with another smaller container filled with water, to place on top of the cabbage to make sure it stays submerged. Let the cabbage soak at room temperature for 2 days.

After 2 days, drain the cabbage, rinse with water and set aside. Meanwhile, make the pickling liquid by bringing the water to a boil. Add the brown sugar, rice and salt, and stir to dissolve. Lower the heat, let the liquid simmer until the rice opens—about 10 minutes—then cool to room temperature. Place the cabbage in a sterilized, lidded glass jar, fill with the pickling liquid (including the rice) and top with the lid. Let the cabbage pickle at room temperature for at least 5 days (it might take longer if you're in a cooler climate). After 5 days, the cabbage can be transferred to the fridge and stored for up to a year.

Ready for the second stage of the pickling.

Ball

Fried Thai Chilies

MAKES ABOUT 2 CUPS

Fried Thai Chilies condiment is used for Kao Soi (p. 95), but it's a great choice to spice up any dish. It has a nice salt-to-spice balance and offers a little more depth than Roasted Thai Chili Flakes (p. 161) alone.

2 c. vegetable oil
4 shallots, chopped
4 garlic cloves, chopped
20 small dried Thai chilies
1 t. salt
1 t. palm sugar

In a deep-frying pan, heat the oil to 350º. Fry the shallots and garlic until golden brown—about 2 minutes. Remove to paper towels but reserve the oil. Add the chilies to the oil and fry until fragrant—about 1 minute. Remove to paper towels, and again, reserve the oil. Place the shallots, garlic, chilies, salt, sugar and 2 tablespoons of the reserved frying oil into a food processor and blend until smooth (scraping down the sides a few times). If the mixture is too dry and becomes hard to mix, add a little more oil. The mixture is supposed to be somewhat chunky. Store in the refrigerator for up to 3 months.

Fried Shallots

MAKES ABOUT 2 CUPS

Fried shallots are handy to have around. I use them in myriad ways—as a crunchy topping for salads, or as an additional flavor dimension for coconut rice (p. 38). Once fried, shallots become rich and sweet with less of an onion bite. They're one of those ingredients that would be delicious on almost anything.

¼ lb. thinly sliced shallots
⅛ t. salt
2 c. vegetable oil

Add the shallots and salt to a bowl and mix. Heat the oil in a deep pot over medium heat. Add the shallots and fry until golden and crispy, about 5 to 7 minutes. Remove to a paper towel-lined plate to drain. Once cooled completely, store in an airtight container in the refrigerator for up to 1 month.

Meatballs

MAKES 30 MEATBALLS

Meatballs have always been, and will always be, a favorite of mine. When I was little, I used to save all my meatballs to the very end of my noodle soup so I could relish them one at a time. Then one day, my uncle ate all my saved meatballs as a joke. This was not funny. I learned to never walk away from my bowl even for a second, and now I protect my precious saved meatballs from any nearby predators. You can use ground pork or beef for this recipe; here I've used pork. Meatballs add an additional layer of flavor and texture to any noodle soup, like my Beef Noodle Soup with Spicy Garlic Finishing Sauce (p. 77).

1 lb. ground pork

2 T. sea salt

½ t. freshly ground white pepper

1 t. minced cilantro root or stems

1 c. crushed ice

Combine the pork with the salt, pepper and cilantro root or stems. Massage the mixture by rolling it toward you and pushing it away—almost like making dough. Add a little bit of crushed ice as you do this. When the mixture is sticky and feels thicker, roll it into 1-inch balls. Boil the meatballs in water until cooked—about 5 minutes. (They will float to the surface when they are ready.) Meanwhile, prepare an ice bath and drop the meatballs into the ice water immediately to cool. (This helps the meatballs have a tender and "springy" texture.) Alternatively, you could add all the ingredients except the ice to a food processor and pulse—adding ice as you go. But don't overmix or the meatballs will be tough! Check the texture as you mix; it should be sticky. Remove the meatballs from the ice water, drain and either use immediately or refrigerate or freeze for later use.

PRO TIP

Pork on the Rocks

Adding ice while mixing the pork and spices helps reduce the heat created by friction. Heat will make the protein in meat denature and cause the meatballs to be tough and hard.

CHAPTER SEVEN

Fusion Is Not a Dirty Word

I don't think I properly understood the term "fusion cuisine" when I began to cook professionally. I mistook it to mean trendy or even co-opted. But I finally realized that fusion is simply the way a cuisine evolves. People have always been nomadic for various reasons, and we've influenced each other along the way with the culture, traditions and food we bring to the table. For example, Thai food is very much a fusion of Indian and Chinese food. To me, fusion is simply a way to have fun and be creative while still staying true to some of the elements of the original cuisine. The recipes in this section are me stretching my wings by embracing ingredients, combinations and methods usually not present in traditional Thai food. I've made these dishes my own, and I invite you to share them with me.

Coconut Shrimp Fritters

with Sweet-and-Sour Dipping Sauce

SERVES 4 AS AN APPETIZER

I love fried shrimp appetizers, but often I can't eat them because of their breading and my wheat allergy. In my classes, I teach students how to make banana fritters—a popular street snack in Thailand—so I thought I'd try shrimp cooked the same way. My students loved them! I like the shrimp to be peeled and cleaned but I leave the tail on as a little handle. (Most people discard the tail afterward, but personally, I like those fried shrimp tails! Try them!) To use this recipe for bananas (or even sweet potatoes), slice lengthwise into ¼-inch thick planks, then cut them into about 4-inch long pieces and follow the recipe.

FOR THE DIPPING SAUCE:

⅓ c. tamarind water (p. 35)

3 T. water

2 t. Roasted Thai Chili Flakes (p. 161)

⅓ c. sugar

½ t. fish sauce

FOR THE SHRIMP:

½ c. rice flour

¼ c. tapioca starch

1 T. sugar

¼ t. salt

½ c. shredded unsweetened coconut

¼ c. sesame seeds

¾–1 c. water

1 lb. peeled, cleaned large shrimp, tails on

4 c. vegetable oil for deep frying

SUGGESTED WINE:

SPARKLING ROSÉ

To make the dipping sauce, place all the ingredients in a small saucepan and bring to a boil. Lower the heat and simmer for 2 minutes. Remove from the heat and set aside.

To make the shrimp, combine the first 6 ingredients (through the sesame seeds) in a medium bowl and stir to mix well. Add the water and stir. Let the batter sit for 10 minutes to thicken. It should have the consistency of waffle batter, but if it looks too thick after 10 minutes, add a little more water. Meanwhile, heat the oil in a medium pot (or use a deep fryer) to 350º. Dip the shrimp into the batter one at a time until covered, shake off the excess then carefully add them to the hot oil in batches of about 6 shrimp per batch. Fry each batch for 2 to 3 minutes until the shrimp start to float to the top. Remove each batch to a plate lined with paper towels to drain. Serve warm with the dipping sauce.

Thai-Style Ceviche

SERVES 4

The first time I had ceviche, it reminded me of a tangy, spicy shrimp dish that one of my dear family friends used to make for me all the time. Whenever she made it, I would just magically walk in her door, as if I had smelled it all the way from my house. When I tried ceviche here in the U.S., it was good, but never quite spicy enough for me. I decided to make a Thai-style version and so far, I've made this dish with sushi-grade tuna, raw shrimp, raw snapper and raw octopus. My favorite versions have been with the tuna, or a mix of tuna and watermelon cubes. You can buy sushi-grade tuna at many natural grocery stores or from your local fishmonger. Leave the fish in the sauce longer if you like the fish "cooked" more. I like mine pretty raw—after just 2 or 3 minutes—just how I would eat my sushi.

3 T. fish sauce

4 T. lime juice

1 t. white sugar

1–3 small fresh Thai chilies, red or green, minced

2 t. cilantro stems, minced

Pinch salt

2 t. minced garlic

1 lb. sushi-grade tuna, cut into ½-inch x 1-inch pieces, about ¼-inch thick

1 T. chopped cilantro

1 avocado, large dice

Put the fish sauce, lime juice and sugar in a bowl and stir to dissolve. Pound together the chilies, cilantro stems, salt and garlic using a mortar and pestle (or mix together by hand) and add to the bowl. Add the tuna pieces to the bowl and gently stir to coat the fish. Fold in the cilantro and avocado and let the mixture sit to your preferred doneness.

SUGGESTED WINE:

CALIFORNIA SAUVIGNON BLANC

Kale Fried Brown Rice

with Sunny-Side Egg

SERVES 2

This dish makes good use of hearty, crisp kale that's abundant here in Texas in the fall and winter. It's one of those humble recipes that shocks with its depth of deliciousness. At Thai Fresh, we serve this as both a lunch and dinner item. Olive oil is not common in Thai cooking, but I like the flavor it brings here.

2 c. brown rice

6 c. water

2 T. olive oil

1 t. minced garlic

2 c. chopped lacinato kale (also known as dinosaur kale or Tuscan kale)

1 T. light soy sauce

¼ c. Pickled Cabbage (p. 165)

3 T. vegetable oil

2 large eggs

SUGGESTED WINE:

AUSTRIAN GRÜNER VELTLINER

Soak the rice in the water for 30 minutes, then cook (using the same water) following the instructions for brown rice (p. 38). Meanwhile, heat a deep sauté pan until hot, turn the heat down to medium-low and add the oil and garlic. Fry the garlic until brown and fragrant—about 10 seconds. Add the cooked rice, kale and soy sauce and sauté until the kale is wilted. Fold in the Pickled Cabbage and turn off the heat. Next, heat a skillet until very hot. Add the vegetable oil and carefully crack in the eggs so as not to break the yolks. Turn down the heat to medium and let the eggs fry until the bottoms are cooked. (The eggs will release naturally after the bottoms are cooked, so don't move them too soon.) Divide the rice-kale mixture into two bowls. When the edges of the eggs are crispy, carefully remove with a spatula and serve one egg over each bowl.

Drunken Linguini Noodles with Calamari

SERVES 2

Drunken Noodles is another Thai street-food staple. People often ask why the dish is called "drunken" since no alcohol is used in the recipe. One theory is that the dish was created to go well with drinks. It began as a blend of Chinese and Thai cuisine—Thai fish sauce and Chinese dark soy sauce were used, then different ingredients were added like Thai chilies (grab those frosty drinks!). Traditionally, holy basil is included, but it can be hard to find in the U.S. and other countries in the West, so you can substitute regular Thai basil. (Incidentally, if you're a gardener, holy basil grows in the same season as Italian basil, but it takes the heat much better and doesn't mind the cold as much.) I've used linguine here for a fusion twist, but you can use any kind of noodle you like.

8 c. water

6 oz. dried linguine

3–5 small fresh Thai chilies, red or green

2 t. minced shallot

2 t. minced garlic

3 T. vegetable oil

4 oz. calamari, cleaned, cut into 2-inch x 1-inch pieces

½ c. chopped yellow onions

3 T. fish sauce

3–4 T. dark soy sauce

1 t. sugar

1 c. loosely packed Thai basil or holy basil

In a large stockpot, bring the water to a boil. Drop in the linguine and boil until al dente—about 8 to 10 minutes—stirring occasionally. Once done, drain the linguine, run it under cold water and set aside. Next, make a paste out of the chilies, shallot and garlic using a mortar and pestle (or combine and mince together). Heat a large, deep sauté pan over high heat. When the pan is hot, turn the heat down to low and add the oil. Add the paste and fry for 10 seconds until fragrant. Add the calamari and stir-fry until it curls—about 1 minute. Add the onions and sauté for 30 seconds, then add the fish sauce, dark soy sauce and sugar. Add the drained noodles and stir-fry until the sauce is completely absorbed. Add the basil at the very end—folding the hot noodles over the leaves for about 30 seconds until the basil has wilted.

SUGGESTED WINE:
FRENCH MUSCADET

PRO TIP

What's the Score on Calamari?

Slit the sides of the calamari open and halve the tube. Score the inside of the tube with a crisscross pattern, then cut it into 2-inch x 2-inch pieces. As the pieces cook, they'll curl and expose the pretty crisscrosses on the outside of the curls.

Massaman Curry with Buttered Toast

SERVES 4

Massaman Curry is largely influenced by Indian cuisine and very spice-forward. The level of sweetness changes as you travel from Southern Thailand to Central, and the addition of fresh herbs like galangal and lemongrass make it consistently recognized as one of the most complex and delicious foods in the world.

FOR THE MASSAMAN CURRY PASTE:

3 shallots

2 garlic cloves

1 t. coriander seeds

1 t. cumin seeds

2 whole cloves

5 large dried red Thai chilies, seeded, soaked in warm water for 15 minutes

1 t. salt

1 t. ground white pepper

1 T. chopped lemongrass

1 T. finely chopped galangal

1 t. makrut lime zest (optional)

2 t. chopped cilantro

1 t. shrimp paste

(continued on opposite page)

To make the curry paste, place the shallots and garlic cloves on a small baking pan and roast in the oven at 350º until slightly charred. Set aside. Toast the coriander seeds by heating a dry frying pan over medium-low heat. Add the coriander seeds to the pan and move them around constantly until fragrant and lightly browned—about 1 to 2 minutes. Remove to a small bowl. Next, add the cumin seeds to the pan and heat until fragrant and lightly browned. Remove them to a separate small bowl and set aside (the coriander and cumin seeds need to be toasted separately because they toast at different rates). Next, toast the cloves until fragrant and remove to another bowl. Using a large mortar and pestle, make a paste by adding the ingredients one at a time, beginning with the seeds and cloves. Continue with the shallots, garlic cloves and chilies—pounding each ingredient until it's broken into small pieces before adding the next one. Continue with the rest of the ingredients until the mix forms a fine paste.

FOR THE CURRY:

2 13½-oz. unshaken cans coconut milk

1 recipe Massaman Curry Paste

2 lb. beef stew meat

1 cinnamon stick, broken in half

2 bay leaves

4 white cardamom pods (these are almost impossible to find, but Indian black cardamom pods work beautifully; however, green cardamom is very strong and should not be used)

2 T. peanuts

4 c. 2-inch Yukon Gold potato cubes

1 medium onion, chopped into bite-size pieces

3–4 T. fish sauce

2 T. palm sugar

¼ c. tamarind water (p. 35)

Thick buttered toast, for serving

Scoop out the cream from the coconut milk cans (halfway down the can; a little over is fine) and place into a medium saucepan. Bring to a boil over medium heat and cook for 1 minute. Stir in the curry paste and mix until smooth. Turn the heat to medium-low and simmer, without stirring, until fragrant and the coconut cream starts to release some oil, about 3 to 5 minutes. (You'll start to see brown/red oil on the surface.) Add the rest of the coconut milk from the cans and bring to a boil. Add the beef stew meat, cinnamon stick halves, bay leaves and cardamom pods and let simmer for 45 minutes. Meanwhile, roast the peanuts on a sheet pan in a 350º oven until lightly browned and fragrant. After the beef has simmered for 45 minutes, add the potatoes, onions and roasted peanuts and let simmer for another 10 minutes. Add the fish sauce, palm sugar and tamarind water. Turn off the heat, remove the cardamom pods, cinnamon stick halves and bay leaves and serve the curry with thick pieces of buttered toast.

PRO TIP

Go for the Gold

Yukon Gold potatoes give a creamier texture to curries, and there's no need to peel.

Thai Fresh Fried Chicken and Waffle

with Tamarind-Lemongrass Syrup

SERVES 4

In Texas, fried chicken and waffles is a huge thing. I usually can't partake, though, because of my wheat allergy. I knew I was missing out, so I created this recipe to kick off our new Sunday brunch menu at Thai Fresh. I swapped out the wheat flour for gluten-free flour, and subbed the dairy with coconut milk. Of course, there had to be a Thai-inspired syrup as the crown jewel, and our Tamarind-Lemongrass Syrup won out in the test kitchen. The result is a light, fluffy waffle with just a hint of coconut. It's the perfect foundation for a piece of crunchy Fried Chicken (p. 111) and takes it to the next level with a generous drizzle of syrup.

FOR THE TAMARIND-LEMONGRASS SYRUP:

1½ c. sugar

6 T. water

6 T. tamarind water (p. 35)

½ stalk lemongrass, tough outer layer removed, bruised with the side of a knife, cut into 1-inch pieces

2 ¼-inch ginger slices, bruised with the side of a knife

1 small fresh Thai chili, red or green, bruised with the side of a knife

FOR THE BATTER:

2 c. plus 3 T. gluten-free flour

2½ t. baking powder

1¼ t. salt

1 T. plus 1 t. sugar

4 eggs

2 c. plus 3 T. coconut milk

½ c. plus 2 T. vegetable oil

¾ t. vanilla extract

FOR SERVING:

1 recipe Fried Chicken (p. 111)

1 recipe cooked waffles

Toasted sesame seeds, for garnish

Cilantro leaves, for garnish

To make the syrup, combine all of the ingredients in a saucepan, bring to a simmer and let cook for 3 minutes. Strain and discard the solids, set the syrup aside and keep warm.

To make the batter, stir together the flour, baking powder, salt and sugar in a large bowl and set aside. In a medium bowl, beat the eggs until fluffy. Add the coconut milk, oil and vanilla to the eggs and mix well. Add the wet ingredients to the dry ingredients and stir well. Refrigerate for at least 4 hours or up to overnight.

While the batter is chilling, make a batch of Fried Chicken and keep warm. Cook the waffles according to your waffle-maker's instructions. Arrange the waffles on a platter, top each with a piece of chicken and drizzle the syrup with a heavy hand. Garnish with toasted sesame seeds and cilantro leaves and serve.

SUGGESTED WINE:

SPARKLING WINE

Thai Fresh Fried Chicken Sandwich

SERVES 8

This recipe was created by our head chef at Thai Fresh, Gary Smith. Gary wanted to create a Thai version of a fried chicken sandwich, so he combined some key elements of Thai food—ingredients that we already had on hand—and made it into a customer favorite. We serve the chicken on a toasted wheat bun with our housemade Spicy Mayo and Spicy Pickles (recipes on following spread). Yum! The pickles need to be made 3 days in advance, so think ahead when putting this crowd-pleaser in your rotation.

1 c. coconut cream
¼ c. fish sauce
¼ c. soy sauce
1 t. Roasted Thai Chili Flakes (p. 161)
1 t. freshly ground black pepper
½ t. salt
¼ c. unsweetened coconut flakes
1 T. chopped cilantro leaves
8 boneless chicken thighs, skin on
1 c. gluten-free flour
2 t. cayenne
4 c. vegetable oil

FOR SERVING:
Toasted buns
Spicy Mayo (p. 186)
Spicy Pickles (p. 186)
Lettuce leaves
Tomato slices

Combine the coconut cream, fish sauce, soy sauce, Roasted Thai Chili Flakes, pepper, salt, coconut flakes and cilantro in a mixing bowl and stir together. Pat the chicken thighs dry, prick them all over with a fork and add them to the bowl. Cover the bowl and marinate the chicken in the refrigerator for at least 2 hours. Meanwhile, mix together the flour and cayenne and place in a shallow plate. Heat the oil in a stock-pot to 350º. Remove the chicken thighs from the marinade and dredge each piece in the flour mix, then carefully add the chicken to the hot oil, 2 pieces at a time. Fry and turn until the chicken pieces brown and start floating to the surface—about 5 minutes on each side. Remove the chicken to a plate lined with paper towels. Serve the chicken on a bun with the Spicy May, Spicy Pickles, lettuce and tomato.

Thai Fresh Spicy Mayo

MAKES ABOUT ½ CUP

½ c. mayonnaise
2 t. lime juice
1½ t. fish sauce
¼ t. minced small fresh Thai chilies
½ t. minced garlic

Whisk all of the ingredients together in a bowl and keep refrigerated.

Thai Fresh Spicy Pickles

MAKES 1 QUART

1 lb. small pickling cucumbers
3 whole small dried Thai chilies
3 garlic cloves, crushed
2 shallots, smashed
1 c. water
¾ c. white vinegar
1 t. white sugar
1 T. kosher salt

Wash the cucumbers and pack them whole in a quart-size mason jar. Fry the chilies in a pan with a splash of oil until fragrant and darker in color. Add the garlic, shallots and chilies to the jar. In a small saucepan, combine the water, vinegar, sugar and salt and bring to a boil. Stir until the salt and sugar are dissolved, then remove from the heat and let cool slightly. Pour the brine over the cucumbers, seal the jar and shake. Let the pickles cool completely on the counter, then refrigerate. Wait 3 days before using.

Thai Fresh Burger

MAKES 4 BURGERS

I will never understand a burger patty seasoned with just salt and pepper; it just doesn't seem right to this Thai cook. At Thai Fresh, Head Chef Gary Smith made this burger for our crew one day and it was so loved, it became our official Thai Fresh Burger. It's available every summer when bell peppers are in peak season. We serve it with our Spicy Mayo and Spicy Pickles (p. 186). The pickles need to be made 3 days before making the burger, so plan ahead if using.

1 lb. ground beef (we use 80/20 local, grassfed beef)

1 t. minced garlic

½ t. minced shallot

¼ t. (or more) minced small fresh Thai chilies

⅓ c. finely diced bell pepper, any color

⅓ c. finely diced yellow onion

⅓ c. finely chopped button mushrooms

2 T. fish sauce

½ t. salt

¼ t. black pepper

FOR SERVING:

Toasted buns

Spicy Mayo (p. 186)

Lettuce leaves

Spicy Pickles (p. 186)

Tomato slices

Onion slices

Stir-fried veggies (optional)

Cheese slices (optional)

Mix together the first 10 ingredients (through the black pepper) until combined. Form into 4 patties and grill to your desired temperature.

To assemble the burger, spread Spicy Mayo on both sides of the bun. Pile the lettuce, tomato, onion, pickles and stir-fried veggies (if using) on the bottom bun. Top with the burger patty and cheese (if using), followed by the top bun.

Low-and-Slow Oven Ribs

with Thai BBQ Mop Sauce

SERVES 2–4

Ever since I first tasted BBQ here in Texas, I've been obsessed with making a Thai version. This is what I came up with! Instead of cooking my ribs over a pit or in a smoker, like most Texans do, my version is hassle-free: I bake them low and slow in the oven, then slather them with enough Thai BBQ Mop Sauce to get all over your face and hands—as it should be.

FOR THE MOP SAUCE:

3 T. vegetable oil

½ c. Red Curry Paste (p. 41)

2 T. palm sugar

2 t. fish sauce

2 makrut lime leaves, sliced into thin ribbons

FOR THE RIBS:

⅓ c. light soy sauce

1 t. palm sugar

2 garlic cloves, minced

1 t. freshly ground white or black pepper

1 T. minced cilantro stems

¼ t. salt

1 rack baby-back ribs (about 2 lb.)

1 recipe mop sauce

SUGGESTED WINE:

FRENCH GAMAY

To make the sauce, heat a frying pan to medium-low heat. Reduce the heat to low, add the oil and when the oil shimmers, add the curry paste. Fry the paste until fragrant, about 30 seconds. Add the rest of the ingredients and stir-fry to mix. Set aside.

To make the ribs, heat the oven to 250º. Combine the soy sauce, palm sugar, garlic, pepper, cilantro stems and salt to make a wet rub. Cover the ribs on both sides with the rub. Wrap the ribs, meat-side down, in aluminum foil and fold to create a tight seal. Place on a sheet pan and bake for 2 hours. Increase the oven temperature to 350º. Open the foil, drain the juice and use a spoon or brush to mop the ribs on both sides with the mop sauce. Place the ribs, meat-side up, over the open foil and bake on the sheet pan for 10 minutes. Remove the pan, mop both sides of the ribs again with the sauce and put back in the oven for another 10 minutes. Repeat 1 more time, then remove and serve with napkins.

Spicy Beef and Yukon Gold Potato Stew

with Sour-Spicy Finishing Sauce

SERVES 4

This is my adaptation of a Southern Thai-style beef stew; kind of a cross between traditional beef stew and the finishing flavors of a lemongrass soup. I like to use Yukon Gold potatoes because they're denser and give a creamy texture to the soup, and I include carrots even though we don't use them much in Southern Thai cooking (they only grow up north where the weather is cooler). The finishing sauce definitely has a spicy edge, so adjust the Thai chilies to your taste.

FOR THE FINISHING SAUCE:

4 T. lime juice

3 T. fish sauce

1 t. white sugar

½–1 t. minced fresh Thai chilies

FOR THE STEW:

4 c. water or Chicken Stock (p. 150)

1½ lb. beef stew meat, cut into 3-inch pieces

½ t. salt

2 c. Yukon Gold potato cubes (1½-inch cubes)

1 c. carrot coins (1-inch coins)

1 c. chopped onion

1 T. cilantro leaves, for serving

To make the sauce, mix together all of the ingredients in a bowl and set aside.

In a stockpot, bring the water or chicken stock to a boil, add the stew meat and salt and simmer for 50 minutes. Add the potatoes, carrots and onion and simmer for another 10 minutes. After 10 minutes, take the stew off the heat, portion into 4 bowls, add the finishing sauce to each and top with the cilantro.

Fried Tempeh and Cucumber Salad

with Lime Dressing

SERVES 4

Tempeh, a fermented soybean cake, is not something I was familiar with until my first year of teaching cooking classes in the U.S. One of my students asked if she could use it in curries and I wasn't sure, so I gave it a try. I actually prefer a firmer-textured protein like tofu when it comes to curries, but I still wanted to give tempeh a chance. I created this dish to enhance and complement tempeh's subtle flavors. The crunch of the cucumber and the boldness of the dressing really sing in this summer salad. If you don't want to mess with frying the tempeh cubes, brush them with vegetable oil and bake at 325º for 15 minutes.

4 c. vegetable oil for deep-frying
4 c. 1-inch x 1-inch tempeh cubes
2 t. minced garlic
1 t. minced fresh Thai chilies
Pinch salt
2 t. sugar
4 T. lime juice
2½ T. light soy sauce
1 t. plus 2 T. minced cilantro stems, divided
6 c. ¼-inch slices of unpeeled cucumber
½ c. sliced cherry tomatoes

Heat the oil in a medium pot to 350º. Fry the tempeh cubes a few at a time until golden and beginning to float to the top. Remove to a paper towel-lined plate to drain. Make the dressing by combining the garlic, chilies, salt, sugar, lime juice, soy sauce and 1 teaspoon of the minced cilantro stems in a bowl. Mix well, then toss the fried tempeh, cucumbers, tomatoes and the remaining 2 tablespoons of minced cilantro stems with the dressing—beginning with half the dressing and adding more, to taste.

PRO TIP

Making Cucumber Spokes

Instead of simply peeling cucumbers, consider using a handheld shredding tool to score the sides lengthwise and make fancy spokes. Available at most Asian markets, the tool is great for shredding root vegetables like carrots and radishes, and fruit like papaya.

Spicy Red Curry Rice Balls

MAKES 25–30 BALLS

I swear this recipe came to me in a dream. I just woke up one day and felt that I needed to make these little appetizers. Now they're part of my trusted rotation for almost every community event I participate in. They can be made well in advance (up to frying) because you freeze them beforehand, and they can stay that way until needed. Most of all, they're a total crowd-pleaser. Be sure to use warm rice because it mixes more easily. The rice balls can be frozen for up to 6 months.

4 c. warm, cooked jasmine rice (p. 37)
½ c. Red Curry Paste (p. 41)
1 T. light soy sauce
2 t. sugar
4 makrut lime leaves, cut into thin ribbons
½ c.–1 c. water
4 c. vegetable oil, for frying
Sweet-and-Sour Sauce, for dipping (p. 158)

Combine the warm rice, Red Curry Paste, soy sauce, sugar and lime leaves in a bowl, and mix with your hands until well combined. (If the mixture is a little dry, add a bit of water.) Have a bowl of water handy to dip your hands into when they get too sticky, and roll the mixture into balls, about 1½-inches in diameter. (I use a small ¾-ounce scooper to help.) Freeze the balls overnight before frying. When ready to fry, heat the oil in a large saucepan or pot to 350º. Fry the frozen balls until golden and starting to float—about 2 to 3 minutes. Drain on paper towels and serve with Sweet-and-Sour Sauce.

Thai Omelet Breakfast Taco

MAKES 2 TACOS

Thai Omelet is another dish that's dear to my heart. Growing up, our family ate it a lot, and it's one of the first things I learned to make. Contrary to the name, it's not a breakfast item in Thailand; we ate it most often at dinner. This dish pairs well with other foods on the table and features an omelet cooked well-done; some like theirs more well-done than others, and some like their omelet fried by adding more oil and letting the edges crisp. This is the version I like best, but experiment and find out what suits you! Even though Thai Omelet is a classic Thai dish, I included it in the Fusion chapter because, instead of serving it with rice, I wrap it in warm flour tortillas, which are not found in Thai cuisine. I created this version when I was a vendor at the local farmers market trying to come up with a breakfast item to sell before the lunch crowd hit. Since I'm in Austin—the breakfast taco capital of the world—I figured putting my beloved Thai Omelet in a tortilla just made sense.

4 eggs

1 T. fish sauce

¼ c. ground pork

1 shallot, thinly sliced

½ c. chopped tomato

3 T. vegetable oil

Warm flour tortillas, for serving

Homemade Sriracha Sauce (p. 159), for topping

Crack the eggs into a mixing bowl and beat well until they are fluffy and the egg whites are completely incorporated (this is very important for a dense omelet texture). Add the fish sauce, pork, shallot and tomatoes and mix well. Heat a frying pan over medium-high heat until hot. (It's okay if the pan gets very hot and begins to smoke—this will help keep the omelet from sticking.) Add the oil and immediately add the egg mixture. Lower the heat to medium and let the omelet fry for 10 seconds. Begin to pull the omelet toward the center of the pan and tilt the pan to let the uncooked mixture fill the empty space. Repeat for all sides until the eggs are cooked on the bottom. Carefully flip the omelet over using a flat spatula to help. If you can't turn it in one piece, don't worry! Simply cut the omelet into smaller pieces and flip them. Let the omelet fry until the eggs and pork are fully cooked, about 2 minutes. When the edges of the omelet are slightly crispy, divide into warm tortillas and top with Homemade Sriracha Sauce.

CHAPTER EIGHT

Gati Vegan Ice Cream

Honestly, Thai Fresh ice creams came about purely by accident. I had bought too many mangoes and they were going to go bad if we didn't do something quickly. An employee suggested ice cream! So we grabbed ingredients we already had on hand, and processed the first batch of Mango-Lime Ice Cream. When that creamy, sweet, fruity ice cream came rolling out of the maker, we were hooked. And bonus: It was dairy-free! I started to brainstorm ingredients; what else could we put in there? The employees and customers were having so much fun creating combos, we just kept adding new flavors. Here are our bestsellers.

Banana and Texas Pecan Ice Cream

MAKES ABOUT 2 QUARTS

Banana is such a complex and flavorful ingredient, especially when cooked. And Texas pecans are sweet, meaty and plentiful in Austin. This is a perfect recipe for Thai Fresh; I can safely say it's my absolute favorite ice cream flavor.

½ c. chopped Texas pecans
6 c. coconut milk
2 lb. bananas, sliced into 1-inch pieces
1¾ c. palm sugar
2 cinnamon sticks
½ t. salt

Heat the oven to 350° and toast the pecans on a baking sheet (or in a dry skillet on the stovetop) until fragrant. Bring the coconut milk, bananas, palm sugar, cinnamon sticks and salt to a boil and let simmer for a few minutes to dissolve the sugar. Turn off the heat and let the mixture cool completely. Remove and discard the cinnamon sticks, blend in a blender then churn according to your ice cream maker's instructions. As the ice cream finishes, fold in the pecans and churn for another 30 seconds.

PRO TIP

Coconut Milk

I recommend Aroy-D brand coconut milk and cream. Many of the other coconut milks from Thailand have a similar consistency, but Aroy-D is one of the only brands that's free of preservatives and additives, such as guar gum.

Golden Milk Ice Cream

MAKES ABOUT 2 QUARTS

This recipe came about due to the popularity of the Golden Milk Latte at Thai Fresh. Using turmeric in a dessert is uncommon in Thai cooking, so many of our employee partners helped guide the way on this bestseller. I would say I've now acquired a taste for sweet turmeric—after all, it's good for you!

5 c. coconut milk
1¼ c. palm sugar
2 T. plus 1 t. turmeric
2 coins ginger, about ½-inch thick each
½ star anise pod
⅛ t. ground ginger
¼ t. black pepper
¼ t. ground cardamom
¼ t. ground cinnamon
¼ t. salt

In a pot, bring all of the ingredients to a boil—making sure to stir occasionally to prevent the sugar and spices from sticking to the bottom of the pot and burning. Reduce the heat, simmer for 3 minutes, then turn off the heat. Strain out the solids and discard, then chill the liquid until at least at room temp. Churn according to your ice cream maker's instructions.

Roasted Hatch Chili and Peach Ice Cream

MAKES ABOUT 2 QUARTS

Creating an ice cream using Hatch chilies was just a happy accident. I needed to come up with a recipe for a Hatch chili party and this was born. The heat from the chilies brings a very subtle burn at the end. If you have a powerful blender, there's no need to peel the peaches—the skin will be pureed and leave a few specs of color throughout. If you'd like to peel the peaches, blanch them in boiling water for 2 minutes, then plunge them into ice water. The peels should come right off. You can find roasted Hatch chilies in the freezer section of most large grocery stores.

5 c. coconut milk
1½ lb. peach chunks, fresh or frozen
1¼ c. plus 2 T. sugar
2 t. lemon juice
2 t. minced roasted Hatch chilies
½ t. salt

Bring all of the ingredients to a boil and let simmer until the sugar is dissolved. Cool completely, then blend the mixture in a blender. Churn according to your ice cream maker's instructions.

Thai Tea Ice Cream

MAKES ABOUT 2 QUARTS

Thai Tea is always a big hit at Thai Fresh, so we rolled the idea into ice cream. Any flavor of tea you like will work, though, as long as it's strong brewed.

6 c. coconut milk

2½ c. coconut cream

3 c. sugar

Pinch salt

2 c. strong-brewed Thai tea (I use ½ c. of Thai tea mix to 3 c. boiling water and steep for 5 minutes)

In a pot, bring all of the ingredients to a boil and then simmer to dissolve the sugar. Remove from the heat and let the mixture cool completely. Churn according to your ice cream maker's instructions.

Thai Coffee Ice Cream

MAKES ABOUT 2 QUARTS

I wasn't sure if coffee would work as an ingredient for ice cream that has a base of coconut milk—would the coconut flavor overpower the coffee flavor? Fortunately, it worked perfectly, and Thai Coffee Ice Cream is now a customer favorite. For the brewed coffee, we use a locally roasted blend, but a blend with chicory or with a deeper chocolate-y flavor, like ones from Columbia or Brazil, would also work great.

6 c. coconut milk

2½ c. coconut cream

3 c. sugar

Pinch salt

2 c. strong-brewed coffee (I use a large French press to brew 1 c. of ground coffee with 3 c. boiling water and let it steep for 5 minutes)

1 t. instant espresso powder

⅛ t. vanilla extract

In a pot, bring all of the ingredients to a boil, then let simmer to dissolve the sugar. Remove from the heat and let the mixture cool completely. Churn according to your ice cream maker's instructions.

Black Sesame Seed
Golden Milk
Pandan Leaf
Chocolate
Black Sticky Rice Horchata
Cookie Monster

Cake Batter
Black Magic
Beet Chocolate Cake
Adzuki Bean
Thai Tea
Matcha

Thai Chili-Lime Ice Cream

MAKES ABOUT 2 QUARTS

This recipe was inspired by a chili-lime ice cream I once had in San Francisco. I decided to create a dairy-free version using Thai chilies, which have a very distinct flavor.

5 c. coconut milk
Pinch salt
1½ c. plus 1 T. sugar
1–2 small fresh Thai chilies, red or green
6 T. lime juice
1 t. lime zest

In a pot, bring the coconut milk, salt and sugar to a boil. Stir to dissolve the sugar, then remove from the heat. Cool the mixture completely. Add 2 cups of the mixture and the Thai chilies to a blender and blend until smooth. Pour back into the remaining cooled mixture. Add the lime juice and zest and stir. Churn according to your ice cream maker's instructions.

Sweet Corn Ice Cream

MAKES ABOUT 2 QUARTS

Corn is a very common ingredient in Thai desserts, but our U.S. customers thought it sounded strange to mix it into ice cream. Once they tasted it, though, they understood why it works so well.

5 c. coconut milk
1 c. corn kernels (fresh is best)
1¼ c. plus 1 T. sugar
1 t. salt

In a pot, bring all of the ingredients to a boil, then let simmer until the sugar is dissolved. Cool completely, then blend the mixture in a blender—leaving some corn kernel pieces for texture. Churn according to your ice cream maker's instructions.

Pandan Ice Cream

MAKES ABOUT 2 QUARTS

Leaves from the tropical plant pandan are used in many Asian dishes for their nutty, vanilla-like aroma and flavor. This quality is great for desserts, but occasionally you'll see pandan leaves in a savory dish, like my Beef Noodle Soup (p. 77). Frozen pandan leaves are available at most Asian markets.

5 c. coconut milk

4 pandan leaves (massage to break the leaves into pieces)

1 c. plus 3 T. sugar

1 t. salt

Place all of the ingredients in a pot and bring to a boil. Reduce the heat and simmer until the sugar dissolves. Remove from the heat, let the mixture cool completely, then blend it in a blender. If there are any larger chunks of leaves left, strain the mixture through a fine-mesh strainer. Churn according to your ice cream maker's instructions.

Mint-Chip Ice Cream

MAKES ABOUT 2 QUARTS

Mint Chip is a classic ice cream flavor. We began by making ours with crème de menthe, but we soon realized that this flavor is a favorite of kids. So, we ditched the alcohol, added spirulina for color and used mint extract for flavor. Perfect.

5 c. coconut milk

2 t. spirulina

2 t. mint extract

1 c. plus 3 T. sugar

½ c. semi-sweet chocolate chips

In a pan, bring the coconut milk, spirulina, mint extract and sugar to a boil, then reduce the heat and simmer until the sugar is dissolved. Cool the mixture completely, then churn according to your ice cream maker's instructions. While the ice cream is churning, place the chocolate chips in a glass bowl and melt slowly in 30-second intervals in the microwave, or place the bowl in a small pot of simmering water and stir until the chips dissolve. (We've found that keeping the chips whole makes them too large in the finished ice cream. Melting the chocolate first creates thinner chunks when frozen). As the ice cream finishes churning, pour in the chocolate sauce and churn for 30 more seconds. Alternatively, you can remove the ice cream from the maker, pour the chocolate sauce onto the ice cream and once the chocolate sauce hardens, break it into smaller pieces and mix in.

Mango-Lime Ice Cream

MAKES ABOUT 2 QUARTS

This is the very first ice cream we ever made at Thai Fresh, so it has a soft spot in my heart. I had an ice cream machine sitting in the corner of the restaurant for the longest time and finally decided to use it—with great success. We've found that using fresh mango makes a big difference in flavor and texture.

5 c. coconut milk

1½ lb. mango chunks, fresh or frozen

1¼ c. plus 2 T. sugar

2 t. lime juice

½ t. salt

In a pot, bring all of the ingredients to a boil and let simmer until the sugar is dissolved. Cool the mixture completely, then blend in a blender—reserving some chunks of mango to add in when the ice cream is finishing. Churn the mixture according to your ice cream maker's instructions. Fold in the reserved mango chunks as the ice cream finishes.

Chocolate Ice Cream

MAKES ABOUT 2 QUARTS

My customers tell me this is the best chocolate ice cream they've ever had—with or without dairy! The key is to use high-quality chocolate and cocoa powder. Simple but best ingredients always do the trick.

5 c. coconut milk
1 c. sugar
¾ c. semi-sweet chocolate chips
½ c. unsweetened cocoa powder
¼ t. plus a pinch salt
¾ t. vanilla extract

In a pot, bring all of the ingredients to a boil and let simmer for a few minutes to dissolve the sugar. Let the mixture cool completely, then churn according to your ice cream maker's instructions.

Thai Basil Ice Cream

MAKES ABOUT 2 QUARTS

This ice cream is adapted from a David Lebovitz recipe. Mine is dairy-free and spotlights Thai basil, which packs a fresh, herbaceous kick that's perfect on a hot Texas day.

5 c. coconut milk
1½ c. Thai basil leaves, lightly packed
1 c. plus 3 T. sugar
¼ t. salt

In a pot, bring all of the ingredients to a boil, then simmer until the sugar is dissolved. Cool the mixture completely, then blend in a blender. If there are pieces of leaves left, either leave them for texture or strain the mixture through a fine-mesh strainer. Churn according to your ice cream maker's instructions.

Sweet Sticky Rice

MAKES ABOUT 3½ CUPS

¾ c. coconut cream
⅔ c. sugar
½ t. salt
1 pandan leaf (or substitute ¼ t. vanilla extract plus ¼ t. hazelnut extract)
2 c. cooked (hot) sticky rice (p. 39)

Heat the coconut cream in a small sauce-pot. Add the sugar, salt and pandan leaf (or extracts) and stir until the sugar and salt have dissolved. Remove from the heat and cool completely. (The coconut mixture can be made a day ahead and cooled in the fridge overnight.) When the sticky rice is cooked and hot, slowly pour a little more than half of the cooled coconut mixture over the rice and stir to mix thoroughly. Add more, if needed, but make sure the rice doesn't become too wet. Cover and set aside for 15 minutes in a warm place.

To assemble the "Ice Cream Dog" dessert shown below, spread the bottom of a hot dog bun with a little bit of room-temperature Sweet Sticky Rice, add the ice cream scoops of your choice (we used coffee, chocolate and thai basil) and top with roasted peanuts.

Head Chef Gary Smith, Jam Sanitchat, Catering Manager Aly Beaujon, General Manager Rebecca Steen

Acknowledgments

I would like to first thank my parents, Banjong and Orawan Sanitchat, for always providing me with love, respect, trust and a great food culture. Thank you, Mom, for always believing in me; and thank you, Dad, for always making me believe in myself.

I would like to thank my family, Bruce and Leo, for allowing me the time to pursue my passion in food and writing. Bruce, thank you for always letting me do what I love, and for believing in it and never questioning it. Thank you, Leo, for always making parenting a beautiful journey.

Thank you to my team at Thai Fresh—without them, I would not have finished this book. Thank you, Gary Smith, Rebecca Thornton, Aly Beaujon, Shelbie Maggio, Dominique Ivory, Seth Bailey, Justin Quirk, Jesper Drlicka, Elizur Castaneda and Caragh Givens for taking care of business and never failing to deliver. Gary, thank you for allowing me to include your recipes in this book. Thank you to the entire staff for your passion and commitment, and for showing up and giving it your all.

This book is the result of a community effort; it's a labor of love and a symbol of the trust the community has invested in me. I would like to thank all of the Kickstarter backers who chipped in to make this book a reality—I could not have done it without you. Special thanks to Laurie Garber, Kevin Conway, Keri Feferman, Harry Simmons, Elizabeth Laurino, John Lash, Monique Capanelli and Lynn Yeldell for your generous contributions.

Thank you to the creative team behind this book: Kim Lane, my beloved editor and friend, I am very lucky to have had you on this team and to call you a friend. Thank you to my copyeditor, Anne Marie Hampshire, for making sure all of the words ended up looking beautiful. Thank you, Julie Savasky, for interpreting my ideas into a gorgeous layout. Thank you, Jody Horton and Whitney Arostegui of Jody Horton Photography, for the amazing photography—you are so talented, kind and simply the best. Thank you again, Aly Beaujon, for being an essential part of the photo shoot—you made it that much simpler and more fun. Thank you, Chris Corona, for your talent creating the video for the cookbook campaign—I couldn't have picked a better person to capture all of the moments. Thank you, new and old friends, who appeared in my video: Sarah Jey Whitehead, Stephanie Aesthetics, Tom Crantoun, Ian Seyer, Elisha Garza and Meredith McCarty—you are all naturals. Thank you to the Holden Brothers, Josh and Nick, for creating the video script and for following me around to make video clips to promote our campaign.

Thank you, Chef Sonya Coté for your lovely foreword. I am honored to know you and to be part of the same food community. Thank you to Rae Wilson, badass winemaker, sommelier, consultant and great friend. I'm so happy your suggestions for wine pairing are in this book.

Finally, a huge thank you to all of my customers for their support throughout this food journey—you've made it absolutely rewarding and enjoyable, and I look forward to coming to work every day. And to all of my students over the last 16 years—your questions, comments and enthusiasm have made me a better teacher and cook. I have learned tremendously from you.

I'm so incredibly grateful to be a part of this community.

JAM SANITCHAT

Index

Note: Italic page numbers refer to photographs.

H

I

J

K

L

M

N

O

P

T

U

W

Y

Bruce Barnes and Jam Sanitchat

Printed at Reliance Printing in China
through Tailored Group
First Edition, 2020

Published by Thai Fresh Press
909 W. Mary Street, Austin, Texas 78704

Distributed by University of Texas Press

ISBN 978-1-4773-2222-2

Library of Congress Control Number: 2020907313

All photography by Jody Horton except for pages 13, 14-15, 26, 34, 36, 45, 74-75, 88-89, 97, 100-101, 148-149, 151, 152, 166-167, 177 and 198-199 by Jam Sanitchat. Photo on page 17 by Shanna Hickman. Photo on page 129 by Poramat Sanitchat.

Elephant line drawing by Rebecca Wood.

Cover and Book Design: Julie Savasky, 508 Creative
Copyediting: Anne Marie Hampshire
Indexing: Kay Banning